THE KEW GARDENER'S GUIDE TO

GROWING CACTI AND SUCCULENTS

THE KEW GARDENER'S GUIDE TO

GROWING CACTI AND SUCCULENTS

THE ART AND SCIENCE TO
GROW WITH CONFIDENCE

PAUL REES

FRANCES
LINCOLN

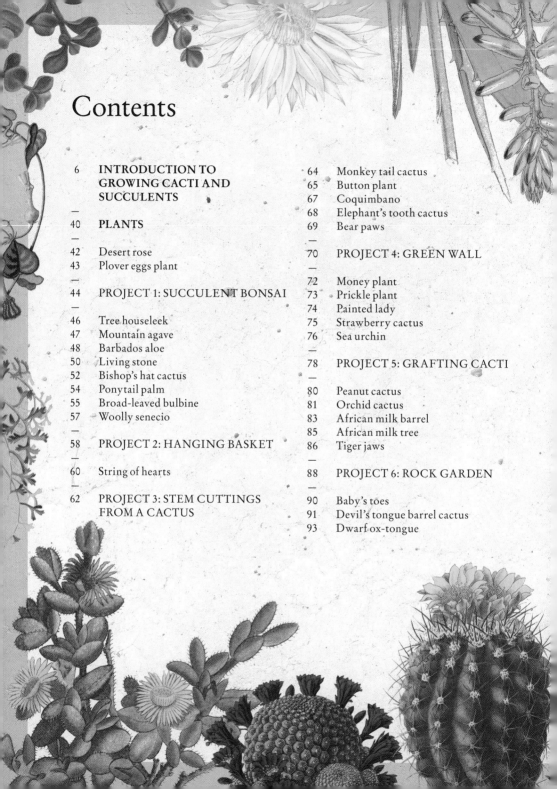

Contents

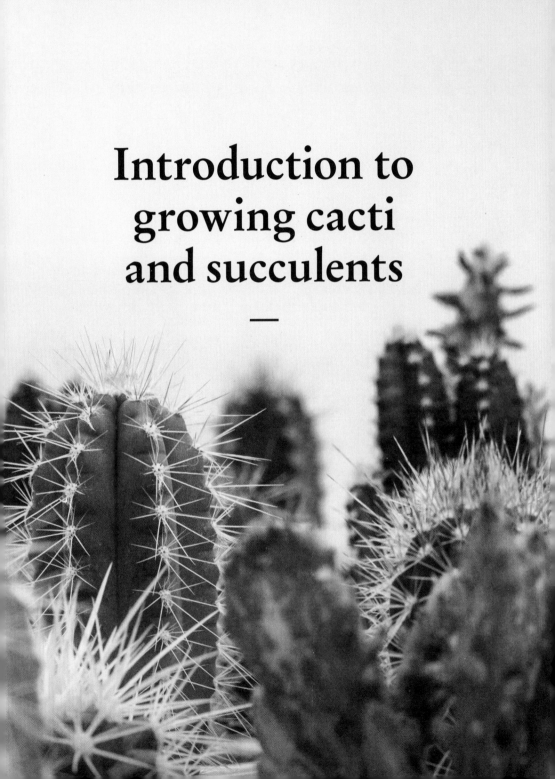

Introduction to growing cacti and succulents

—

THE VALUE OF SUCCULENT PLANTS

As a young boy I remember going to the local garden centre with my mother and seeing the strange succulents growing in small pots at the till. It was there that I received my first tiny succulent plant. It was not long before I inevitably managed to overwater it through too much love. Upset by the loss, we made another trip to the garden centre to find a replacement. Eventually, I started to work out what succulents needed, and my plant began to flourish. Needless to say, one plant became two and before I knew it I had caught the bug and had a bit of 'succulent fever'.

Succulent plants have a wonderful diversity. Succulence can be found in about sixty different plant families and across over 650 genera within those families, but the majority of succulent plants are found within four families: Aizoaceae, Cactaceae, Crassulaceae, Euphorbiaceae. They have an amazing ability to fascinate people – maybe because they are such oddities, being unlike other plants. I suppose you could say they are a little alien. This is true in some way when you consider the arid environments where they grow: they are from another world or at least not one most people are familiar with. They defiantly capture the imagination with their unique forms, colours, textures and ability to adapt and survive the harsh environments they live in. Add all these factors together in a small, decorative terracotta pot and you have the perfect pot plant – interesting, decorative and thriving (for the most part) on neglect. It's not hard to see how these plants capture our imagination and, for some of us, they become an absorbing hobby.

Succulents have always been popular plants to grow but, in recent years, with

OPPOSITE A sunny spot in the house is perfect for a cluster of potted succulents.

This impressive display was created for an open day in the Tropical Nursery at the Royal Botanic Gardens, Kew.

the increasing amount of information on social media including about rare species, they have become a fashionable craze and a bit of an obsession for some people.

A succulent plant can be defined as any plant that has the ability to store water within its tissues, and the word 'succulent' is derived from the Latin word *sucus* (juice), which refers to this characteristic. Where succulents store water can differ between species: some do so in their leaves; others in their stems; while yet more conserve water in their roots – or sometimes in a combination of these places. Based on this characteristic, succulents can be very loosely divided into leaf succulents, stem succulents and root succulents.

The large majority of cacti are leafless stem succulents, with the exception of a few species that have semi-succulent leaves. As well as their succulent stems, some cacti also have a thick tuberous

and succulent taproot to help them withstand dry periods.

The fact that all cacti store water means that they can all be classed as succulents. It is, however, worth remembering that, although cacti make up a large percentage of species considered succulent, not all succulents are cacti. Succulent *Euphorbia*, like cacti, are largely stem succulents and mostly leafless – and some have succulent roots, too. Meanwhile, Aizoaceae and Crassulaceae are leaf succulents – some with succulent stems and a few with succulent roots.

How succulent a species is largely depends on the environment in which it grows naturally. Succulents from harsher environments will have the ability to store more water and withstand longer periods of drought compared to species that grow in less arid environments.

Types of succulent plants

Leaf succulent

Gibbaeum dispar

Root succulent

Lophophora williamsii

Stem succulent

Euphorbia polygona var. horrida

Columnar cactus

Stenocereus thurberi

Epiphytic cactus

Rhipsalis spp.

Globular cactus

Echinocactus grusonii

Shrubby cactus

Opuntia microdasys

Trailing or clumping cactus

Cleistocactus winteri

Pieter van Wyk (SANParks) and Alex Summers (Cambridge University Botanic Garden) are seen here documenting succulents in the Richtersveld, South Africa.

WHERE DO SUCCULENTS GROW?

The first answer that jumps to mind is deserts, and it is true that deserts around the world hold a high diversity of succulent plants. However, cacti and succulents can also be found growing in a wide range of other places.

What their habitats have in common is a lack of water, at least for periods of the year – the length of time that these areas experience drought differing considerably. The largest desert in the world is Antarctica, where there is plenty of water but it is mostly frozen. The very arid desert environments in which some cactus and succulents grow receive very little rainfall throughout the year: for example, the Atacama Desert in South America is considered one of the driest places on the planet and gets an average of 15mm/½in of rain per annum; and the Richtersveld in South Africa receives less than 200mm/8in per annum yet it is considered a biodiversity hotspot. Within these extreme environments, succulents often take advantage of ecological niches, where they try to avoid the harsh conditions by growing under the protection of larger shrubs or in between rocks or boulders. Many species nestle at the bases of nurse plants: for example, the saguaro cactus (*Carnegiea gigantea*) is protected by a nurse plant when young. Other succulents may flourish in quartz gravel plains, where the quartz crystals reflect sunlight, thereby keeping the ground cooler and conserving moisture. Succulents often prefer the cooler slope of a mountain, and may also thrive in dunes, where they make the most of coastal fog or dew. Coastal regions also attract succulent species that enjoy shallow soils on rocky cliffs or the saline conditions, which reduce the availability of water for most types of plants.

Succulent Aizoaceae are dotted across this pink-quartz gravel landscape.

These *Cheiridopsis* flowers open in bright light and close later, as the sun sets.

The vast landscape of the southern African deserts can prove quite humbling. Rocky outcrops such as this often contain a high diversity of botanical treasures nestled in the rocks.

Seasonally dry areas that at certain times of the year may have high rainfall, yet have periods with little to no rain too, provide a suitable environment for some succulents. When at high altitude, these habitats generally experience high winds, shallow soil, cooler or freezing temperatures, where succulence may be advantageous. Other situations where you may find succulent colonies are in areas such as shallow rocky soils within rain shadows of mountains or places protected by other plant species with the succulents growing epiphytically.

Spot the *Argyroderma* concealed among the stones in the quartz flats of the Knersvlakte.

Where you can see succulents

The best place to start is at your local botanical garden, which is bound to have an array of succulents on display: for example, the Princess of Wales Conservatory at the Royal Botanic Gardens, Kew houses a large variety of species, as does the succulent collection in the Botanical Garden, University of Zurich, Switzerland. Look out for shows or join your local cactus and succulent club. These groups often have events or meet-ups where you can see and talk about succulent plants. Or next time you are booking a holiday why not go and see them in their natural habitat. Visit the arid Namaqualand in South Africa, for example, or the deserts of Arizona and Mexico.

The Princess of Wales Conservatory at the Royal Botanic Gardens, Kew contains an arid zone, which provides the optimum conditions for the succulents growing there.

HOW HAVE THEY ADAPTED?

Cacti and succulents have unique physiology that allows them to grow naturally in often hot and dry environments. Such plants absorb water when available, and then store it within water-storing cells found in their leaves, stems and/or roots. In addition to this ability to store moisture for times of scarcity, many species have developed other ways to survive in harsh environments: for example, they often have reduced leaves or, in some cases, no leaves at all, and so rely on chlorophyll in their stems for photosynthesis. This adaptation reduces the surface area where water can be lost through transpiration.

The skins of cacti and succulents are often thick and waxy, which is very effective at retaining moisture and preventing water loss. They can be grey in colour or have red hues and tints. Grey-coloured plants are often from areas with high light levels or that experience hot, dry conditions. This colouring helps reflect light and keep the plants cooler and, in turn, reduces moisture loss. These grey-coloured plants also tend to grow more slowly, which means they use less water. Many succulents turn reddish at times; this is often due to high light or drought conditions. Changing colour helps protect the plants from sunburn, and also means that they will grow more slowly, therefore needing less water.

TOP RIGHT *Echinopsis spiniflora*
CENTRE RIGHT *Rhipsalis elliptica*
BOTTOM RIGHT *Echeveria pulvinata*

Like all plants, succulents absorb carbon dioxide through stomata (minute pores) in their leaves and stems, in order to photosynthesize. Opening stomata in arid environments can cause unnecessary water loss, so unlike other plants most succulents keep their stomata closed during the day and open them at night, storing carbon dioxide in the form of malic acid to be used during the daytime. This process is referred to as crassulacean acid metabolism (CAM) photosynthesis. In some cases when night temperatures remain high, CAM plants can undergo a process known as CAM idling, during which the stomata will remain closed in the night as well as the day, recycling carbon dioxide from respiration.

Cacti and succulents often develop sunken stomata. Such a characteristic is very beneficial as it reduces transpiration. The air around the stomata is less exposed to the wind, leaving the humidity higher around the stomata and reducing the movement of moisture from the inside of the plant to the outside.

Hairs and spines have multiple functions on succulent plants. Like sunken stomata, they reduce transpiration and they are well adapted to harvesting moisture from mist, fog, rain and condensation, too. Moisture droplets on these hairs and spines are channelled down the plant, accumulating near the roots. The spines on cacti also act as protection, preventing herbivory.

It is often thought that the root systems of plants that grow in desert environments are deep; however, this is true for only a select few species. Most succulents tend to be shallow rooted. Being closer to the surface, the roots can make the most of moisture events such as light rain, mists, fogs and condensation at night.

Oreocereus celsianus

Parodia scopa

Parodia magnifica

Conophytum minutum, Crassula deceptor and
C. hemisphaerica

THREATS WITHIN NATURAL SUCCULENT HABITATS

Despite the resilience of cacti and succulents to survive in some of the world's most hostile environments, they cannot always adapt to the rapidly increasing man-made pressures. As a result, an alarming number are at risk of extinction in their natural habitats. A study by the International Union for Conservation of Nature (IUCN) reported in October 2015 that an estimated 31 per cent of the 1,478 cacti species evaluated were threatened with extinction. Unfortunately, this is also true for many other succulent groups. The increased extinction risk is being driven by a number of factors including urban expansion, overgrazing, habitat exploitation and mining. Such persistent pressures alongside ever-increasing effects of a changing climate will lead to many of these plants becoming extinct in the wild.

One particular concerning threat to many species is over-collection of these plants from habitat, to supply the global ornamental trade – the rate of poaching having risen significantly over the years (see Poaching, page 23). Sometimes the origins of one plant's popularity can be traced. For example, in 1897 Professor Peter MacOwan collected a strange rounded plant from an area near Graaff-Reinet in South Africa. He sent the plant to the Royal Botanic Gardens, Kew, where in 1899 it flowered for the first time and in 1903 was named *Euphorbia obesa* by Sir Joseph Dalton Hooker. After its discovery, its uniqueness resulted in over-collection for the horticultural trade, driving the species to the brink of extinction. Today, it is still a much sought-after plant and sadly there are probably more plants growing in collections than there are in the wild, where it is considered endangered.

Conservation

Several cacti and succulent groups are protected and prohibited from being traded across borders without permits, as part of the Convention on International Trade in Endangered Species of Wild Fauna and Flora (CITES). The CITES-listed species include almost all cacti, *Aloe* and many succulent *Euphorbia*, *Pachypodium* and Didiereaceae. Botanical institutions around the world such as The Huntington and the South African National Biodiversity Institute (SANBI) are working hard to protect and restore these species in their natural habitats, as well as to conserve them in *ex-situ* collections. Seeds of many species are stored in the Royal Botanic Gardens, Kew's Millennium Seed Bank at Wakehurst, Sussex. This seed bank is the largest *ex-situ* plant conservation programme in the world, and forms part of a global partnership in the race to ensure no plant species goes extinct. There is nothing more special than seeing these strange plants in their habitats for the first time. Hopefully, with a joint effort we can ensure they will grow for generations to come.

This collection of *Pilosocereus* species, including *P. quadricentralis*, is growing in the Tropical Nursery at Kew and has yet to be stored in the Millennium Seed Bank.

WHERE TO GROW SUCCULENTS AT HOME

Succulents can make great house plants if given the right conditions. One of the most important factors to consider is the light levels in your home. Most species will thrive if given a bright spot on a windowsill, but ideally not in direct sunlight in summer. In autumn and winter, many species undergo a dormant period, when they will need less light. However, when plants are actively growing you should supply higher light levels, to ensure etiolation does not occur.

As your collection expands, and if you want to grow a wider range of species, a greenhouse will provide the best growing conditions. This should have a good base, such as concrete or bricks, and a damp-proof membrane. Position the greenhouse in the sunniest part of your garden, to increase available light and heat. The larger the greenhouse, the more stable the temperature will be.

Ventilation is important to control temperatures as well as to reduce humidity, so helping to keep pests and fungal pathogens at bay. Automatic

Many cacti and succulents grow well in a suitably positioned windowsill planter (here filled with *Haworthiopsis attenuata*, *Parodia leninghausii* and *Kalanchoe tomentosa*).

Behind the scenes in the Tropical Nursery at the Royal Botanic Gardens, Kew, is a glasshouse filled with a large conservation and reference collection of cacti and succulents.

ventilators can be useful, as they open and close automatically depending on the temperature required.

Electric fans will also improve air circulation. In summer, shading may be required; this can be in the form of 40 per cent shade cloth or else a greenhouse shading paint brushed on to the glass.

In winter, insulate your greenhouse with bubble wrap or horticultural fleece, to help keep it frost-free. Use an electric fan heater, oil radiator or propane

heater for plants that need warmer temperatures than this.

A conservatory is also another option for growing cacti and succulents at home. Always position such plants in the sunniest spot and provide good ventilation in hot weather.

Depending on where you live, it may be possible to grow a range of more tolerant species outdoors year-round. Species selection is an important factor here; often plants can survive

Hardy succulents grow in free-draining soil in the rock garden at the Royal Botanic Gardens, Kew.

comparatively cold temperatures provided they are protected from winter rainfall (see individual plant profiles for optimum conditions, pages 40–135). Cultivate more tolerant succulents in pots or plant them in a rock garden in a free-draining soil.

Echeveria pulvinata

CHOOSING AND BUYING SUCCULENTS

Always buy your plants from a reputable source where the plants are ethically and legally obtained. The best place to start is local garden centres, which often have a variety of cacti and succulents for sale. When choosing your plants, check that they are healthy and not etiolated; if in doubt, don't purchase them.

Unfortunately, many retailers label their plants as cactus or succulent rather than providing a species name. Therefore, if you are looking for named species and more choice, use a local specialist succulent nursery. If the succulent bug has truly bitten, join your local cactus and succulent society, which can provide expert advice and often has plant sales or swops.

Always be careful when purchasing succulents from online platforms. Even though it is illegal to collect plants from their natural habitats without permission, too often plants poached from the wild are sold online. Frequently, seeds of rarer species fetch high prices; however, once germinated, the seedlings may not be the species or variety advertised. Also, when buying plants online, be sure you are aware of all the regulations, especially if the plants are being shipped from abroad. Plants found without the correct documentation such as a phytosanitary certificate and CITES documentation will be confiscated and destroyed.

Poaching

The increase in popularity of succulent plants and particularly in the demand for rare succulents have caused poaching to become a significant problem, with collectors going to extreme lengths to obtain rare plants. The unscrupulous removal of these species can have a devastating effect on the natural populations of these amazing plants. As growers of these beautiful oddities, we all have a duty of care to ensure that they have a future. Therefore, when buying cacti and succulents, avoid supporting the illegal trade in poached plants.

Huernia zebrina

Care needs to be taken when stacking terracotta pots.

Always select a container that is the appropriate depth for the plant or plants that you will want to grow in it.

EQUIPMENT

Pots

There certainly is a lot of choice when it comes to pots, and there are many good options, each with pros and cons. Therefore, when selecting the right pot to grow your plant in, consider the following points: drainage; pot material; and pot shape and size. Whichever pot you choose, any excess water must be able to drain out of the bottom.

The next decision is between a plastic or terracotta pot – both materials being suitable for growing succulents. Terracotta pots are more decorative; are porous, which helps them dry out quicker; and can keep roots cooler. They are, however, more expensive than plastic; may need more watering; are harder to repot; are harder to clean and store; and easily broken. Plastic pots are widely available; come in a broader range of shapes and sizes than terracotta; are easy to clean and store; and need less frequent watering but may stay damp longer during dull, cooler weather.

The shape and size of the pot is important, too. Many growers like to use square pots, to maximize bench space. Pot depth is another significant consideration as many succulents are shallow rooted. Therefore, choosing a pot that is not too deep is essential, especially as the plant gets larger and needs repotting. Some species, however, may prefer a slightly deeper pot.

Tools should be kept clean and sharp.

It is best to keep succulents a little constricted and pot on only when needed, into a slightly larger pot. Overpotting will result in the potting compost staying wet longer than optimal and in turn can lead to your plant rotting (see page 141).

Other essentials
- Brushes – for cleaning any sand off your plant after potting; a small brush is handy for pollination or dipping into alcohol for removing pests (see page 140).
- Gloves – for protecting your hands from spines when repotting.
- Hand lens – for taking a closer look at your plants and spotting pests early.
- Labels – for identifying plants, especially when your collection starts to grow.

- Propagator – for seed sowing (see pages 34–7).
- Root hook – for loosening soil from root balls.
- Secateurs – for pruning.
- Sharp knife or scalpel – for taking stem cuttings (see page 37).
- Sieve – for sifting compost.
- Snips – for removing dying flowers and stems.
- Tongs – for handling spiny plants when repotting or taking stem cuttings.
- Trowel or scoop – for lifting soil and compost during potting.
- Tweezers – for trying to remove spent flowers, bits of gravel from between the spines or the occasional spine in a finger.

POTTING COMPOSTS AND SOILS

When growing succulents outdoors, ensure the plants have sufficient drainage. Depending on your soil type, you may need to add sand and grit. Consider creating a raised bed or rock garden, where an aggregate or pumice drainage layer can be added and the planting pockets filled with a suitable succulent potting mix.

When it comes to potting compost, every grower you speak to will use a different mix with slightly different components. Choosing a succulent mix is down to what suits your growing conditions and the range of species you wish to cultivate. Succulents come from areas where there is generally very low organic matter in the soil, which is, therefore, prone to drying out quickly. The worst enemy of any succulent plant is waterlogged soil. Therefore, the potting mix must be free-draining with a low organic content.

Most succulents do well in a sandy succulent potting soil such as a mix of equal parts soil-based potting compost, horticultural sharp sand and 3–4mm/$1/8$–$1/6$in washed potting grit. Avoid peat-based compost where other sustainable options are available. Ingredients you can add to your compost for extra drainage include pumice, lava rock, molar clay or cat litter, perlite or akadama. Species that come from drier habitats or that are more prone to root rot may require a higher percentage of drainage material (see individual plant profiles, pages 40–135). Remember some of the more tropical or epiphytic species prefer a slightly more organic mix.

PLANTING

Remove the plant from its old pot and gently tease away any loose growing medium. Inspect the roots for pests and root rots (see pages 136–41); remove any dead roots, being careful not to damage the major roots. Dust any damaged roots with a fungicide, sulphur or charcoal powder. Fill a pot with fresh potting compost of an appropriate mix (see Potting composts and soils, left). Insert the plant into the compost at the same depth it was previously growing, then firm it without compacting.

Brush any compost off the newly potted plant and pick out any grit from among the spines or leaves. Some growers use grit for topdressing, unless the plant (e.g. *Fenestraria*, page 90) is from, for example, a sandy area, in which case they may opt for coarse silica sand. Although a topdressing looks appealing and can help stabilize the newly potted plant, it may be difficult to see if the compost below is wet or dry. Label your newly potted plant and note the date of potting on the back.

WATERING

After planting, leave the plant dry for a week or two, to allow any damaged roots to callus and heal, before watering. Then water cautiously initially, to encourage new root growth.

Be aware of water quality – too much calcium can cause problems such as calcium deposits on your plant and in time may build up in the compost. Therefore, check the composition of

Ensure you have all the tools and materials needed before starting to plant or repot. A clear working area and clean tools minimize pests and diseases.

Watering can be done from above or below the container. When watering from above, remove the rose so you can direct the water at the roots and avoid getting the top of the plant too wet.

your tap water, as it could have a high level of calcium and be slightly alkaline. If you use tap water, you may need to repot your plant a bit more frequently. Rainwater is ideal, but be careful to exclude organic debris from the collecting tank, as it could cause disease.

A 'less is more' approach is often best when watering cacti and succulents; after all, they are well adapted to survive periods of drought. However, some species are more capable of coping with water stress than others, and although many plants grow in very arid regions this is not true for all succulents.

As a rule of thumb, most plants should be watered as temperatures and light levels increase. Water cautiously at

first, encouraging plants to come back into growth. As they do so, increase the quantity of water by thoroughly wetting the potting compost and then allowing sufficient time for it to dry out before rewatering.

For watering purposes, plants can be divided loosely into winter growers, summer growers, drought-dormant species and all-year growers. The watering regimes for winter growers such as *Conophytum* and some succulent *Pelargonium* generally starts in autumn and stops towards the end of spring. In summer, they should be kept dry and allowed to go dormant; this is how these species evade hot dry seasons. As a general rule, for summer

Pachypodium succulentum

Conophytum chrisocruxum

growers such as most cacti and *Agave* watering should start in spring and cease in late autumn, to allow for winter dormancy. Other species such as *Pachypodium* are drought dormant and will go into dormancy when water is withheld; most growers choose to stop watering these during winter months. Other cacti and succulents such as epiphytic cacti and many *Crassula* will require year-round watering.

Some species including many cacti may have two dormancy periods. In these cases, plants are kept dry all through the winter and are watered from spring to autumn except in midsummer, particularly if night temperatures stay high. When temperatures are high at night, the growth rate may slow so these plants need less water while they cope with the temperature stress.

Other factors to consider when watering include: the type of potting compost – some mixes dry out faster than others; and the size and type of pot – compost in a large pot will take longer to dry out than in a smaller one, and compost in a terracotta pot dries faster than in a plastic pot. How well rooted your plant is can also be an important factor: the compost around a well-rooted, pot-bound plant will dry faster than around a freshly potted or overpotted plant. Consider the position of your plant and how much sun it gets:

the same plant in a shady spot will not dry out as quickly as one in bright light. Too much light will also cause plants to experience light stress and slow their rate of growth. Airflow will reduce humidity and help dry compost faster.

Temperature is another variable to consider: a plant in a cool greenhouse or on a windowsill near a radiator will have different watering needs. Always think about how the weather and cloud cover, temperature and humidity will affect your plant's response to watering.

Overwatering can cause root rot (see page 141), especially when cacti and succulents are watered at the wrong time of year or during unfavourable conditions. Other plants may absorb more water than they can store, resulting in them becoming overly inflated or in some cases bursting. This is often seen in some stone plants (*Argyroderma, Lithops* and a few other genera in Aizoaceae) and ribbed cacti.

Underwatering – although easier to rectify and not as serious as overwatering – can still cause problems. Underwatered plants will lose the moisture reserves needed to sustain them through dormant periods, may go into dormancy prematurely and, in worst-case scenarios, will shrivel up and die.

FEEDING

Although in most cases succulents survive long periods without any feeding, to keep healthy they do require some nutrition. Nitrogen (N) is for growth, phosphorus (P) promotes root development and potassium (K) encourages flowering. A good-quality general or foliar fertilizer will include micronutrients such as magnesium and other trace elements important for healthy plants.

Buy low-nitrogen fertilizers for succulents. Too much nitrogen can cause plants to grow too quickly, resulting in weaker plants more susceptible to pests and disease.

During the growing season, apply a general fertilizer at half the recommended rate, or else use a specifically formulated cactus and succulent fertilizer. A monthly feed will be suitable for most plants, especially at the start of the growing season; then stop feeding them towards the end of the growing season. Don't overfertilize your plants.

REPOTTING

Many succulents are slow growing and can survive for years in the same pot and compost, but to keep them healthy and growing well you should repot each plant when it has outgrown its pot, or every 3–5 years. For tips on planting see page 26.

Repotting is best done early in the growing season, when the plant is coming into growth. This may be spring for summer growers or autumn for winter growers. Although it is possible to repot winter-dormant species in winter, in these instances it is important to ensure the compost remains bone dry till spring. In cases where the old potting mix is very different from the new mix or very compacted, it may be worth gently teasing away all the old compost.

Potting grit or coarse silica sand can be used to topdress a repotted plant (here, *Echinocactus grusonii*).

PRUNING

Most cacti and succulents rarely if ever require pruning because of their slow and often compact growth. For faster-growing or shrubby species such as elephant bush (*Portulacaria afra*) and cranesbill *(Pelargonium paniculatum)*, light pruning may be needed to keep plants in shape. During the growing season, remove any unwanted branches with a pair of sharp secateurs or a knife. Small bushy succulents such as *Delosperma* and *Cotyledon tomentosa* may from time to time need a light prune to keep them in shape.

Succulent climbers such as *Hoya* may require some growth control from time to time. Prune back new growth but leave any flowering stems as these will produce blooms in the future. Other climbers may die back when they go dormant; during this time prune away all their dry stems.

Some genera may become too tall for the spaces where they are growing, so you may need to reduce their heights. Cutting the tops off columnar cacti will encourage them to sprout lower down and the removed stems can be used to start other plants (see Stem cuttings, page 37). Also, many columnar cacti, succulent *Euphorbia* and species like ponytail palm (*Beaucarnea recurvata*) can take some time to branch, and pruning them can encourage multiple branching. When pruning *Euphorbia* be careful of its white latex, which can be a skin irritant.

Echeveria derenbergii is quick to offset and soon fills a pot. In spring and summer, it will bloom en masse.

In the tree houseleek (*Aeonium arboreum*), the inflorescence develops from the central growing point of the rosette and after flowering the rosette dies; it should then be pruned off. In some succulent species, however, the dying inflorescence forms a cage around the plant and protects it from herbivory. For these species, leaving the inflorescence is preferable.

In some cases, pruning is required to remove diseased or damaged stems, to prevent the spread of pests and disease and to help create a more appealing plant.

HOLIDAY CARE

Succulent plants are well adapted to endure periods of drought, which means they are easy to leave when you go away. However, before departing, and particularly in the growing season, give your plants a good water. Most succulent species will survive a couple of weeks without further watering. If you go away for any longer, you may need to ask a friend or neighbour to water your plants. Be sure to give clear and simple instructions.

In addition to watering succulents in a greenhouse, someone will have to open and close vents in summer, and check to ensure the heating is working in winter.

Give plants growing outdoors in summer a good soak, which should keep them going until your return.

Pollination

It can be very rewarding to raise new plants from seed collected from your own plants, but before you can harvest seed you need to pollinate your plants. Pollination is essential for the survival of plants, which go to great lengths to ensure that they attract pollinators. Succulents are no exception. Some produce bright white flowers, which open at night to attract bats; and others bear bright red, tubular flowers to entice birds; yet more succulents create a foul scent to lure flies; and many more produce an abundance of flowers in different colours to tempt insects.

Arrojadoa penicillata's short-lived flowers are bird pollinated so need hand pollination indoors.

Although some species can be self-pollinated, many need pollen to be transferred from another plant. To ensure that no unwanted hybridization occurs on the plant from which you want to take seed, isolate the flowers to exclude potential pollinators. A fine mesh bag does the job. When the flowers are open, transfer pollen from one plant to the stigma of another, using a small paintbrush. After pollinating, replace the bag back over the pollinated flower and label it with the date and parent plant. If successful, the ovaries will start to swell and set seed.

When sowing seed collected from your own plants, remember that fleshy fruits often contain a germination inhibitor. Clean the seeds thoroughly and soak them in water to remove any inhibitors.

Parodia magnifica produces brightly coloured flowers to attract pollinators (here, a hoverfly).

The fruit of *Echinopsis huascha* splits to expose the fleshy inside pitted with tiny black seeds.

PROPAGATION

Propagating succulents from seeds, cuttings, division (of offsets), layering and grafting can be very rewarding and, in most cases, is easy to do. It is a great way to increase your collection or share it with others.

Seed

Fresh seed is always better than older seed, so ensure you get it from a reputable supplier. The best time to sow is in spring, when light levels are improving, and the temperature is warmer during the day. If you need to start sowing earlier in the growing season, use a propagator and grow light.

Mix equal parts sand, fine grit and sifted seed compost. Sterilize this seed compost mix before sowing seeds, by pouring boiling water over it or by placing moistened compost in a microwave for 2–5 minutes. Fill individual pots or seed trays with the cooled sterilized mix, leaving a 1cm/½in gap between the compost and the top of each pot. Then gently press down, ensuring the mix is firm but not compacted.

Sow the seeds on the surface of the compost (one species per pot), being careful to distribute the seed evenly and not too densely. When sowing, it is important to avoid crowding seeds as the subsequent seedlings may be in the same pot for some time. Lightly press the seeds, ensuring they are in contact with the compost.

Place a sealed polythene bag over a newly sown pot to retain moisture while germination occurs.

Then place each pot in a propagator and keep moist until the seeds germinate; if the surface dries out, spray with sterilized water. Rather than using a propagator, some growers place pots in sealed polythene bags and remove them only once the seedlings are well formed – this is likely to take up to a year later, in spring. Cacti do well with this method, but other succulents should be removed from the higher humidity of a polythene bag soon after germination. Most seeds should germinate in 7–28 days.

Some seeds may undergo dormancy, so if your seeds don't germinate at the first attempt allow them to dry out and re-wet them later – or even the following spring.

Covering the seeds lightly with fine silica gravel will allow light to reach the seed and also help to keep the seeds humid, thereby assisting gemination. Never use any other covering material, as most succulents require light to germinate. Label each pot with the sowing date, plant species, seed source and seed catalogue number. Then place each pot in a tray of sterilized water (cooled boiled water will suffice). Some growers may add a preventative fungicide at this stage.

Allow the water to soak in until the surface of the compost is moist. After watering, lightly spray over the surface with sterilized water and fungicide to ensure the seeds have good contact with the compost.

These seedlings of *Neobuxbaumia euphorbioides* are ready to be pricked out into a larger tray or individual pots.

These two-year-old seedlings were well spaced when pricked out into large trays.

Other species such as colder-growing *Opuntia* may need cold stratification to germinate; this involves putting the moistened seed pots in a cooler environment for a week or so before bringing them into the propagator.

Establishing germinated seedlings is the next challenge. Spray the seedlings lightly so they do not dry out; if overwatered at this stage you may encourage moss and algae. Allow the surface to dry out a little to reduce the risk, but be careful not to desiccate the tiny seedlings. Also, keep them covered or lightly shaded, for example by using a piece of horticultural fleece, because it is important that they are not exposed to high light levels, which may cause them to turn a red colour and slow down their growth rate.

Once the seedlings are a bit bigger, topdress the compost lightly with sand or fine grit, to deter moss and algae. Fungus gnat (see page 138) can also be problematic, especially for young seedlings. If you sterilize your compost and keep each pot well covered, you can exclude fungus gnat.

Gradually acclimatize the seedlings to less frequent watering and lower ambient humidity. Once they can be easily handled, usually after a year's growth, prick out the seedlings into individual pots or space out in larger seed trays. During their first year out of the propagator, seedlings should be kept a little warmer, at 14°C/57°F, and be watered throughout the year while they establish.

Vegetative propagation
Stem cuttings

Many succulents can be grown from stem cuttings, which are usually taken early in the growing season once plants have had enough time to replenish their moisture reserves.

Make the cut at a joint, where the wound would be the smallest. If this is not possible – particularly with cactus species – bevel the base of the cutting so that it does not become concave as it dries. Cuttings can be anything from 2–3cm/¾–1¼in to over 1m/39in long. Apply sulphur or charcoal powder to the cut surface to help dry the wound and protect it from rot. Rooting powder will serve the same purpose.

Stand each cutting upright in a deep pot, with the cut surface resting on a layer of grit or pumice spread over the base of the pot. Leave in a dry, shaded place for a day or two so that the wound can callus over. Stem

Each cacti cutting needs to callus before it is planted into an individual pot.

This *Pilosocereus* cutting is well calloused and is starting to form roots, so nearing planting time.

Having been left to dry out of direct light, this *Echeveria derenbergii* cutting can now be planted.

cuttings from large columnar cactus or *Euphorbia* may need more than a month for the wounds to heal.

Keep an eye on the cuttings to ensure they are drying. If you see any rot developing, immediately cut back to healthy material or discard the stem cutting and take a fresh one.

In time, the cut surface will harden over and may even start producing root initials. At this stage, your cutting is ready to be potted up. If transferring your cuttings into individual pots, choose small, shallow ones, so you can monitor rooting activity easily.

Plant each one in sharp sand or a free-draining potting soil (see Potting composts and soils, page 26). Water lightly, keeping the potting medium moist but never saturated; allow it to

dry thoroughly before moistening it again. Once the cuttings have rooted, slowly increase watering and transfer each young plant into a larger pot.

Leaf cuttings
Some succulents can be started from leaf cuttings, which are very easy to do (see also page 128). The downside to starting new plants from leaves is that it can take longer to get larger plants, compared to growing them from stem cuttings (see page 37). It's worth considering which method is suitable for your situation.

Leaf cuttings are best taken in spring after the plants have had a good water and the leaves are full of moisture. Carefully remove plump, healthy leaves cleanly from the stem. Push each leaf cutting slightly into a tray of lightly moistened, sandy succulent potting soil (see Potting composts and soils, page 26) to help the roots make contact. Then place the tray in indirect light, and lightly mist over occasionally.

Roots will start to form at the base of each leaf, followed by a small plantlet. The leaf will eventually wither, while a small plant develops in its place. Once it is big enough, prick it out and plant into an individual pot.

Division

The quickest way to produce new plants is by dividing some of your larger ones. The ideal time to do this is while repotting.

Remove the mother plant from its pot and gently tease away any offsets. Discard any dead or damaged roots, and dust wounds with sulphur powder. Transfer each offset into its own pot and leave it dry for up to a week, before watering.

Layering

This is a great way of growing new plants, especially for succulents that creep and naturally root along their stems. Fill a pot up with free-draining succulent potting mix (see Potting composts and soils, page 26), place the pot next to the mother plant and pin the stem to be layered into the top of the compost with a piece of wire, and water the new pot. Thereafter, keep the compost lightly moist. Once the stem is well rooted, cut the layer away from the mother plant.

Species like string of hearts (*Ceropegia woodii*) form tubers at the nodes of the stems; layering this species will help tubers to develop.

Grafting

Grafting is a technique in which one species is attached to another in a way that they eventually fuse together. This type of propagation has a number of benefits: the growth rate of slow-growing species can be increased by grafting them on to more vigorous root systems; grafting can make tricky species easier to grow; and grafting on to winter-hardy rootstock can increase the cold tolerance of borderline cold-hardy species.

This technique (see page 78) is best done in late spring and summer, when both the rootstock and mother plant are in active growth.

Once this *Haworthia cymbiformis* has been removed from its pot, it can be carefully teased apart into smaller clumps, which are then planted up individually.

Plants

—

Desert rose

Adenium obesum

The desert rose is a very architectural plant that forms a succulent trunk with a swollen base, giving it an appearance of a miniature African baobab tree (*Adansonia digitata*). It is deciduous, losing its leaves when the dry season arrives. It often flowers *en masse*, with vivid pink, tubular blooms. Desert rose is widespread throughout Africa, where it grows in warm, seasonally dry and rocky environments.

—

WHERE TO GROW

Grow in a terracotta pot in a sandy, free-draining potting mix in a conservatory, greenhouse or beside a sunny window. In summer, this species can be moved outdoors, but be careful it does not burn in direct sunlight. It doesn't tolerate the cold very well and is best kept above 10°C/50°F in winter.

—

HOW TO GROW

The thick succulent roots prefer to be a little restricted, so avoid overpotting desert rose. Water regularly when in growth, but be careful not to overwater as this species can easily rot if the potting mix is not allowed to dry out. Feed once a month with a balanced fertilizer. In winter, reduce watering and allow this succulent to drop its leaves while light levels and temperatures are low. Propagate from large stem cuttings or truncheons (see page 37), or from seed (see page 34).

—

GROWING TIP

Try growing desert rose in a shallow bonsai pot (see pages 44–5), where some of the roots can be exposed and trained.

Family
Apocynaceae
Height and spread
1–3x1.5m/3–10x5ft
Temperature
12–35°C/53–95°F
Position
Bright light
Flowering time
Spring–early summer
Pests
Mealybug, mildew, red spider mite

POISON ARROWS
All parts of desert rose are toxic. It has been used traditionally in Africa to poison arrowheads for hunting.

NOTABLE CULTIVARS
- 'Arctic Snow' bears brilliant white, frilly flowers.
- 'Arrogant' is a real showstopper with its yellow-throated, red flowers.
- 'Black Emperor' produces large red flowers tipped almost black.

Plover eggs plant

Adromischus cooperi

This great little succulent gets its common name from its spotted leaves, which bear a likeness to plover eggs. It is native to the Eastern Cape in South Africa, where it thrives in cracks on rocky slopes. Its slow growth and compact habit make it an ideal plant for a small pot.

WHERE TO GROW

Plant in a small, shallow terracotta pot in a free-draining potting mix, or add to a mixed planted bowl (see South African mini-desert, page 106). Although it tolerates reduced light levels, plover eggs plant prefers a brighter position.

HOW TO GROW

Give frequent light watering in summer, with a heavier one once a month; ensure the soil dries out well before watering again. Reduce watering in winter and avoid getting the foliage wet. Plover eggs plant propagates very easily from leaf cuttings (see page 38).

GROWING TIP

Place your plover eggs plant in a location where it won't be moved or bumped much, because the leaves are very fragile and break off easily. This vulnerability can be great if you want a leaf cutting, but frustrating if you are trying to grow a specimen plant.

Family
Crassulaceae
Height and spread
7x15cm/3x6in
Temperature
5–30°C/41–86°F
Position
Bright, indirect light
Flowering time
Summer
Pests
Mealybug

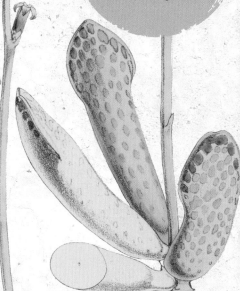

BLUSHING RED IN SUN
The leaf colour of plover eggs plant depends on how much light it gets. Plants in strong light will develop a reddish blush, while those in lower light levels will be greener.

OTHER NOTABLE SPECIES
- *A. maculatus* is slightly larger than *A. cooperi*, and produces attractive, marbled, flat, fleshy leaves.
- *A. marianiae* is a very variable species. The form often named *A.m.* f. *herrei* has bizarre, rough, cylindrical leaves tinged red.

Succulent bonsai

The largest growing succulent species must be the African baobab (*Adansonia digitata*), which can reach 25m/82ft. This strange tree can store vast amounts of water within its massive succulent trunk. In winter, it loses all its leaves and looks as if it has been planted upside down. Unfortunately, growing a plant to this size is not possible at home. However, you can capture the spirit of a large succulent tree by training a succulent as a bonsai. The art of growing bonsai is to plant a suitable species in a shallow pot and in time train it to give the illusion that it is older and larger than it really is.

Many succulent species make great bonsai and my favourite must be the desert rose (*Adenium obesum*, see page 42). It forms a thick succulent stem easily. In its natural habitat it is often found growing in shallow, rocky soils, making it ideal for a shallow bonsai pot. It can be trained to grow over rocks or be lifted to expose the top of its fleshy root system. Apart from its great architectural form, the bonus to growing this species is that it flowers freely with spectacular pink blooms.

SUCCULENTS SUITABLE FOR BONSAI
Adansonia digitata
Adenium obesum
Crassula arborescens, C. ovata
Portulacaria afra
Tylecodon paniculatus

1. Feed some bonsai wire through the drainage holes in a shallow pot or bonsai pot. Then place a bit of mesh over each drainage hole.
2. Remove your plant (here, *Crassula arborescens*) from the pot and carefully tease out the roots from the soil.
3. Place a bit of free-draining potting soil in the base of the pot.
4. Position your plant in the pot and spread out the roots.
5. Anchor the plant with the bonsai wire.
6. Fill in the pot with the remaining potting soil, add any decorative stones and then topdress.
7. Water the pot, then move it into a suitable place indoors.

Tree houseleek

Aeonium arboreum

Tree houseleek grows naturally in Gran Canaria and Morocco in shallow soil on rocky slopes close to the coast. It forms a multi-stemmed shrub with each stem crowned by a rosette of succulent leaves.

WHERE TO GROW

Ideally, plant in a free-draining, sandy potting mix, although this species is not fussy, as long as it does not stay wet for extended periods. Tree houseleek likes high light levels but can tolerate semi-shade too. It will do well beside a sunny window or in a conservatory, as well as outdoors. Bring indoors during colder months.

HOW TO GROW

Feed regularly in the growing season with a low-nitrogen fertilizer. Water deeply when it is in growth and allow the soil to dry before rewatering. Reduce watering in midsummer when temperatures are high, as tree houseleek will go into a summer dormancy and watering during this time can cause blistering on the leaves. Water cautiously in midwinter, when light levels are poor. Tree houseleek may require light pruning to keep it in a good shape. Propagate from stem cuttings (see page 37).

GROWING TIP

If your plant starts to produce lots of aerial roots it could mean there is a problem such as rot (see page 141) or compacted or stale potting soil.

Family
Crassulaceae
Height and spread
1–2x0.5m/3–7x1½ft
Temperature
8–30°C/46–86°F
Position
Bright light
Flowering time
Summer
Pests
Mealybug

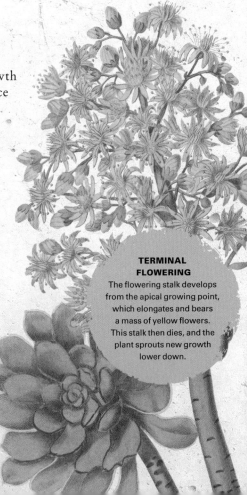

TERMINAL FLOWERING

The flowering stalk develops from the apical growing point, which elongates and bears a mass of yellow flowers. This stalk then dies, and the plant sprouts new growth lower down.

ANOTHER NOTABLE SPECIES AND CULTIVAR

- *A. tabulaeforme* forms a plate-like rosette flat against the soil or cliff face in its habitat.
- *A.* 'Zwartkop' is a classic, dark-leaved cultivar; be sure to give it enough light to get the best colour.

Mountain agave

Agave montana

This striking plant has a rosette of tough, olive-green leaves with red teeth on the margins and sharp terminal spines. When it reaches flowering maturity, an asparagus-like growth, to 4m/13ft high, emerges from the centre of the plant and bears several pendent, yellow flowers.

—

WHERE TO GROW

Mountain agave grows well in a conservatory in full sun, in a pot filled with a mix of nine parts free-draining potting compost and one part organic matter. Being one of the hardiest of all the *Agave* species, your plant can also grow outside in a free-draining soil or in a rock garden (see page 88).

—

HOW TO GROW

Water well in the growing season; reduce watering in autumn and keep dry in winter. Feed with low-nitrogen fertilizer in summer. Every 2–3 years, repot mountain agave and remove any dead roots and older dried leaves at the plant base. Propagate from seed (see page 34).

—

GROWING TIP

Although mountain agave is a cold-hardy species it is often the combination of wet and cold that can be detrimental to its growth. Therefore, ensure good drainage and try to protect it from winter rain, especially during its establishment.

Family	Asparagaceae
Height and spread	1.5x1.5m/5x5ft
Temperature	−15–5°C/5–41°F
Position	Bright light
Flowering time	Summer
Pests	Mealybug, scale insect

LEAVE AN IMPRINT
When the leaves of mountain agave unfurl from their tightly wrapped growing points, imprints are left by the previous leaves, thereby creating an interesting pattern.

Barbados aloe

Aloe vera

Of the nearly 600 different species of *Aloe*, which can be found growing in a variety of habitats from the cape in South Africa to the Arabian Peninsula and Madagascar, Barbados aloe is by far the most popular. It suckers from the base, has lime-green succulent leaves with toothed margins and spikes of yellow pendent flowers.

—

WHERE TO GROW

Although it can tolerate light frost, in cold climates it is best to grow this species indoors in a pot in bright light or in a conservatory, or bring it indoors in the colder months. Barbados aloe likes a well-drained, soil-based potting mix with added grit and will cope with semi-shade.

—

Family
Asphodelaceae

Height and spread
80x80cm/32x32in

Temperature
5–30°C/41–86°F

Position
Bright light–indirect light

Flowering time
Winter

Pests
Aloe mite, aphid, mealybug, scale insect, vine weevil

USE WITH CAUTION
The clear gel in the *Aloe vera* leaf is often used in beauty and health products, while the yellow latex just below the leaf surface is toxic and can cause skin irritation and abdominal cramps and diarrhoea if consumed.

HOW TO GROW

Water year-round, but substantially reduce watering in midwinter. Ensure that the potting compost is completely dry before rewatering. Avoid getting water in the crown of the plant as this can lead to rot. Repot every 2–3 years, removing all soil and pruning off dead roots. After repotting, do not water for a week or two. Most aloes grow well from stem cuttings (see page 37) or division (see page 39).

GROWING TIP

The flowers produce copious amounts of nectar, which drips on to the lower leaves. Wipe these clean, to avoid sooty mould.

Aloe zubb

ANOTHER NOTABLE SPECIES AND GENUS

- *A. humilis* (Spider aloe) is a small aloe that forms clusters of grey heads.
- *Aloiampelos striatula* is a climbing aloe that is hardy to –5°C/23°F.

Living stone

Argyroderma testiculare

Living stone is an unusual plant with a single pair of grey, egg-shaped succulent leaves. It grows in the quartz-gravel plains of southern Africa, where it blends into its surroundings. This small plant is slow growing and doesn't require much space, and its flowers emerge between each pair of fleshy leaves in autumn.

—

HOW TO GROW

Argyroderma are winter growers and should be watered sparingly in summer. Like *Lithops*, they tend to split if overwatered. When the new leaves are emerging in winter, stop watering to allow the moisture reserves from the old leaves to be recycled into the new leaves. Start watering again when the new leaves lose turgidity. Feed with a half-strength, high-phosphorus fertilizer monthly in autumn. Propagate from seed sown in autumn (see page 34).

Family
Aizoaceae
Height and spread
3x6cm/1¼x2½in
Temperature
8–30°C/46–86°F
Position
Bright light
Flowering time
Late autumn
Pests
Mealybug

KEEPING COOL
The quartz-gravel plains where living stone grows reflect sunlight and help to keep the soil and roots cool. The gravel reduces evaporation from the soil below, too.

Living stone blends in well when grown among quartz gravel.

WHERE TO GROW

Grow near a sunny window or in a greenhouse, in a small, shallow pot filled with a mix of one part soil-based potting compost, one part sharp sand and one part 3–4mm/⅛–⅙in potting grit. Position the plant where it will get as much light as possible. If you take it outdoors in summer, protect it from the rain.

—

GROWING TIP

Dressing a pot with quartz gravel will not only look decorative and natural, but will also help to stabilize the plant.

Argyroderma delaetii

ANOTHER NOTABLE SPECIES

- *A. fissum* is smaller, with narrower leaves forming small clumps in time.

Bishop's hat cactus

Astrophytum myriostigma aka Living rocks

The bishop's hat is a solitary and spineless cactus. It is slow growing, but with time can reach 60–100cm/24–39in. Its grey body has pronounced ribs, which grow in a perfect star formation, and is spotted with many white, hairy scales. Yellow flowers are produced in the centre of the plant in summer. Bishop's hat cactus is native to the highlands of Mexico, where it grows on steeps calcareous alluvial slopes. It is sometimes called living rocks due to its ability to mimic surrounding rocks.

—

Family
Cactaceae

Height and spread
60–100x20cm/24–39x8in

Temperature
5–30°C/41–86°F

Position
Bright light

Flowering time
Late spring–early summer

Pests
Mealybug, scale insect

IT'S IN THE NAME
The botanical name *Astrophytum myriostigma* is derived from Greek words *aster* (meaning 'star'), *phyton* ('plant'), *myrios* ('countless') and *stigma* ('points') – thus, the star plant with many spots.

WHERE TO GROW

Although bishop's hat cactus can tolerate relatively low temperatures, it cannot cope with winter humidity. Fill a small terracotta pot with a very free-draining potting mix, such as one part sand, one part 4mm/$\frac{1}{6}$in pumice and one part soil-based potting compost. Adding one part limestone grit to the mix will also help mimic its natural conditions. Position near a sunny window or in a greenhouse above 5°C/41°F.

—

HOW TO GROW

Bishop's hat cactus is slow growing and can be trickier to grow than some other cacti. It is susceptible to rotting and needs to be watered only sparingly through spring and summer. Keep completely dry in winter. A monthly low-nitrogen feed in spring and summer will help speed up growth. Increase the pot size only slightly as the plant grows. Propagate from seed (see page 34).

—

GROWING TIP

If in doubt, do not water this plant. Less is more when it comes to this tricky cactus.

Astrophytum ornatum

Astrophytum asterias

OTHER NOTABLE SPECIES

- *A. asterias* is spineless and has white, fussy patterning and white, yellow or pink flowers (see also What is a planter?, page 120).
- *A. capricorne* has attractive, long, interlaced spines.
- *A. myriostigma* var. *nudum* is an unspotted form.
- *A. ornatum* produces long spines and white banding patterns on its solitary succulent stem.

Ponytail palm

Beaucarnea recurvata aka Elephant's foot

This slow-growing evergreen can reach a height of 8m/26ft when planted outdoors in the ground in ideal conditions; however, it is likely to stay smaller if cultivated in a pot. Over time, the lower part of the trunk swells to form a bulbous caudex. Although ponytail palm superficially looks like a palm, it is not related to true palms.

—

WHERE TO GROW

Plant in a pot filled with a mix of four parts soil-based potting compost and one part grit or pumice, to aid drainage. Ponytail palm prefers full sun to light shade, which makes it ideal near a bright window or in a conservatory. It can be moved outdoors in summer, but bring it indoors in winter, especially if conditions are wet and below 10°C/50°F.

—

HOW TO GROW

This species is very drought tolerant and can go without water for extended periods. Water in summer, ensuring sufficient time for the soil to dry out completely before watering again. Water sparingly in winter, but avoid the compost staying too wet for prolonged periods. Feed monthly with a low-nitrogen fertilizer in summer. Propagate from seed (see page 34).

—

GROWING TIP

The ponytail cactus has a terminal inflorescence, which will branch only after it has flowered. To encourage it to branch before flowering, prune off the tip of the stem in spring.

ANOTHER NOTABLE SPECIES

- *B. stricta* has grey foliage and a fissured swollen caudex.

Family	Asparagaceae
Height and spread	5x1m/16x3ft
Temperature	10–28°C/50–82°F
Position	Bright light–semi-shade
Flowering time	Summer
Pests	Mealybug

COMMON YET RARE
Although ponytail palm is common in cultivation, it is threatened with extinction in its natural habitat in Mexico.

Broad-leaved bulbine

Bulbine latifolia

This stemless, aloe-like succulent has soft green leaves forming rosettes 30cm/12in across. Unlike most aloes, it has no teeth on the leaf margins. It is a reliable flowerer, producing feathery yellow blooms on spikes over 50cm/20in long. Broad-leaved bulbine grows naturally in rocky gorges in the Western Cape in South Africa.

—

WHERE TO GROW

This species is a fantastic addition to a rock garden (see Rock garden, page 88), although it is not frost tolerant so bring it indoors in colder climates. It also makes a good pot plant if given a bright location and a mix of four parts free-draining soil-based potting compost, one part grit and one part sifted composted bark. Keep it out of direct sunlight especially in summer, but ensure some light reaches the plant; if not given enough sunlight, it can quickly etiolate.

—

Family
Asphodelaceae
Height and spread
20x50cm/8x20in
Temperature
5–30°C/41–86°F
Position
Bright light
Flowering time
Late winter–spring
Pests
Mealybug

DEVIL IN THE DETAIL
Bulbines are closely related to *Bulbinella* but are easily distinguished by their fluffy anthers.

HOW TO GROW

Broad-leaved bulbine can be thirstier than most succulents, so water regularly in spring and summer. In autumn and winter, water sparingly and keep the soil on the dry side. Feed with half-strength balanced fertilizer monthly in spring. Repot every other year into fresh potting mix. When repotting, remove any old leaves and cut off any dead roots. Divide older offsets from the mother plant (see Division, page 39).

—

GROWING TIP

When repotting, always position broad-leaved bulbine a little deeper in the pot than previously. New roots will then develop higher up the stem.

Bulbine latifolia

OTHER NOTABLE SPECIES

- *B. frutescens* makes great ground cover and will quickly fill a pot.
- *B. mesembryanthoides* is a little trickier to grow, but very rewarding with its flat, translucent-tipped leaves almost level with the soil surface.

Woolly senecio

Caputia tomentosa aka Cocoon plant

Woolly senecio is a curious, generally slow-growing shrub with cylindrical succulent leaves covered in silvery white, woolly hair. In summer, it produces yellow flowers, and it makes a great feature plant in a decorative pot.

—

WHERE TO GROW

Grow in a free-draining, nutrient-poor mix such as one part soil-based potting compost, one part sharp sand and one part 3–4mm/ ^{1}/8–^{1}/6in potting grit. Although it can cope with low temperatures, woolly senecio will not tolerate wet and cold weather together. It is best grown in a conservatory or near a bright window. In summer, move woolly senecio outdoors, where it can enjoy air movement. In an appropriate climate, it also does well in a rock garden (see page 88).

—

HOW TO GROW

Woolly senecio is very drought hardy and can go for long periods without water throughout the year. It does well, however, if watered well in spring and summer, allowing the potting compost to dry out completely before rewatering. Reduce watering in autumn, and then water lightly and infrequently in winter. Keep the foliage dry in winter. Give a monthly, low-nitrogen feed in summer; alternatively, add slow-release fertilizer to the potting mix when planting. Increase the pot size only slightly, if needed, when repotting. Take stem cuttings, 5–7cm/2–3in long (see page 37). Seeds are rarely available, mainly because woolly senecio is not self-fertile.

—

GROWING TIP

Occasionally mist the foliage during favourable weather. When the foliage is wet, the silvery hairs become translucent, exposing the chlorophyl beneath. Always keep woolly senecio dry in winter.

OTHER NOTABLE SPECIES
- *Curio repens* (blue chalksticks) has bluish grey, cylindrical leaves.
- *Kleinia stapeliiformis* has strange, snake-like stems with striped, white patterning

Family
Asteraceae
Height and spread
15x50cm/6x20in
Temperature
5–35°C/41–95°F
Position
Bright light
Flowering time
Summer
Pests
Aphid, mealybug (especially while flowering)

USEFUL ADAPTATION
The woolly hairs covering the leaves do a great job of reflecting sunlight and keeping the plant cool in hot weather. They also encourage fog and dew to condense on the plant, helping it to harvest moisture and to conserve it during warmer dry periods.

Hanging basket

Pendent succulents are ideal candidates for growing in hanging baskets, as many cremnophyte (cliff-loving) species can be found in their natural habitats dangling from the cracks and crevices of rocky outcrops. A hanging basket allows these plants to grow as they would do in nature. Succulent species that scramble along the ground and among rocks also look good spilling over the edge of a hanging basket, as do epiphytic cacti, which grow naturally suspended from tree branches.

When creating a succulent hanging basket, be creative and find your perfect combination of well-rooted, healthy plants. You could choose a single plant species and in time grow an impressive hanging specimen or you could opt for a combination of species that complement each other. You may decide to use only hanging plants or to include some upright species, too. When choosing a variety of species, you must consider their individual cultural needs: they should all have similar water, light, soil and temperature requirements. Also bear in mind the weight of the hanging basket once filled with potting compost and the plant or plants; to keep it lighter, include perlite or pumice rather than potting grit in the potting compost.

SUCCULENTS SUITABLE FOR A HANGING BASKET
Cleistocactus winteri subsp. *winteri*
Cotyledon pendens
Epiphyllum
Rhipsalis
Schlumbergera
Sedum morganianum

1. Line a sturdy hanging basket with coir matting to keep the soil in the basket.
2. Using scissors, trim the liner neatly along the top of the basket.
3. Place some relatively light, free-draining potting mix in the base of the basket and then insert your plants (here, *Cleistocactus winteri* subsp. *winteri*).
4. Fill in the gaps with potting mix.
5. Attach chains and hang your basket in its new home.

String of hearts

Ceropegia woodii

The string of hearts is an evergreen trailing species with grey-green, heart-shaped leaves held on thin stems, which can grow to 40cm/16in long. Small tubers form at the base of each stem and along the stems at the nodes. The distinctive purple flowers, although small (2cm/¾in), are tubular with bulbous bases. The top of each flower is funnel-like with frilly petals fused to form a cage over the opening. String of hearts occurs naturally in the eastern parts of southern Africa, where it thrives in rocky locations in forest habitats.

—

WHERE TO GROW

Grow in a hanging basket or trail over the edge of a pot on a windowsill. Plant in a mix of one part soil-based potting compost, one part of sifted organic matter and one part potting grit. Do not overpot string of hearts as this could result in the potting mix staying too wet, leading to rot (see page 141).

—

Family
Apocynaceae

Height and spread
10x200cm/4x79in

Temperature
10–28°C/50–82°F

Position
Indirect light–semi-shade

Flowering time
Summer

Pests
Mealybug

CAPTURING POLLINATORS
Each flower on string of hearts attracts small flies, which are enticed by the fragrance. They enter and move through to the bulbous base, where they get trapped by the downward-pointing hairs in the floral tube. While trapped, they encounter pollinia (pollen). The flower then starts to fade and the hairs wither, releasing the pollinator and allowing it to carry fresh pollen to the next flower.

HOW TO GROW

Water regularly in summer, allowing the potting compost to dry out before watering again. In winter, occasionally water lightly if the plant looks thirsty. Give a monthly half-strength feed in summer. Propagate by taking stem cuttings (see page 37), preferably with tubers attached, or else place stem cuttings with four or five nodes in water; they should root in a week or two.

GROWING TIP

Keep a watchful eye out for mealybugs (see page 138), which often hide underneath the tubers and eventually cause root loss and rot problems (see page 141).

ANOTHER NOTABLE SPECIES

- *C. fusca* has grey succulent stems and vibrant red flowers; it is endemic to the Canary Islands.

Stem cuttings from a cactus

Stem cuttings are a great way of growing new plants. When you have enough material, this method allows you to produce a larger plant faster than you would be able to using leaf cuttings (see page 38) or growing plants from seed (see page 34). Occasionally, your plants may become a bit leggy or too large, and stem cuttings can be a useful way to start new plants to replace the older plant eventually with smaller, more compact specimens. Another reason for growing new plants from stem cuttings is in order to share such plants with friends.

SUCCULENTS SUITABLE FOR STEM CUTTINGS

Cereus spp.
Cleistocactus spp.
Echinopsis/Trichocereus spp.
Espostoa spp.
Myrtillocactus spp.
Opuntia spp.
Oreocereus spp
Pachycereus spp.
Pilosocereus spp.
Selenicereus spp.

1. Remove the cactus-stem cutting at a joint or (as here, on *Trichocereus macrogonus* var. *pachanoi*, aka *Echinopsis pachanoi*) through the stem, with a hand saw.
2. After cutting through the stem, use a sharp knife to bevel the cut end in order to prevent the cut surface from becoming concave.
3. Treat the wound with sulphur or charcoal powder.
4. Place the cutting upright in an empty pot, with pumice or grit in the base.
5. Move the pot to a dry, shaded place while the wound calluses; this may take several days or a couple of weeks, depending on the size of the cutting. Once callused or root initials are noticed, pot up your cutting (see Stem cuttings, page 37).

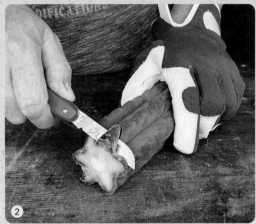

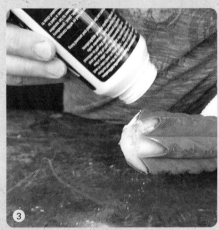

Monkey tail cactus

Cleistocactus winteri subsp. *colademono*

The monkey tail cactus is endemic to Bolivia, where it hangs from the sides of steep cliffs. The pendent stems are covered with soft, greyish white hairs, and they look and feel like tails. Be careful, though – beneath the soft hairs are sharp spines. In summer, red flowers form down the length of the stems, putting on quite a show.

WHERE TO GROW

Grow in free-draining cactus compost in a hanging basket (see page 58) or a pot where the stems can trail over the sides. Although monkey tail cactus can cope with cooler temperatures, it must be kept completely dry in winter and protected from rain. Place in a bright location but keep out of direct sunlight.

HOW TO GROW

Water every week or two in spring, depending on weather conditions; allow the pot to dry out thoroughly before rewatering. During the warmest periods of summer, keep the compost on the dry side. Reduce watering in late autumn and keep the compost dry in winter. In the growing season, give a monthly feed with a half-strength fertilizer low in nitrogen and high in phosphorous and potassium. Repot every 2–3 years. Propagate by stem cuttings (see page 37) or seed (see page 34).

GROWING TIP

To get good flowering from your plant in summer, monkey tail cactus needs a dry and cool dormancy period in winter.

OTHER NOTABLE SPECIES

- *C. straussii* has similar, greyish white hairs, but is much larger and upright in habit compared to monkey tail cactus.
- *C. winteri* subsp. *winteri* (golden monkey tail) is another pendent species, but has golden yellow spines.

Family
Cactaceae

Height and spread
200x5cm/79x2in

Temperature
5–28°C/41–82°F

Position
Bright, indirect light

Flowering time
Late spring–summer

Pests
Mealybug, red spider mite, scale insect

TALE OF A MONKEY
The scientific subspecies name *colademono* comes from the Spanish *cola de mono*, which translates as tail of the monkey, alluding to the tail-like form with white, fur-like spines.

Button plant

Conophytum bilobum aka Pebble plant

This small, compact, clump-forming plant has a shallow root system and yellow flowers, which develop in autumn through the centre of the two fused and lobed leaves. In summer, button plant becomes dormant and its outer leaves dry out to form a papery sheath around next season's new leaves. It is a native on the shallow rocky slopes in arid regions of the Northern Cape in South Africa.

WHERE TO GROW

Plant in a shallow pot filled with a mix of two parts sand, two parts soil-based potting compost and one part sifted organic compost. In the growing season (autumn to late spring), place button plant in a cool greenhouse or on a bright windowsill; in summer, when dormant, this species does not need as much light.

Family
Aizoaceae

Height and spread
5x15cm/2x6in

Temperature
10–25°C/50–77°F

Position
Bright, indirect light

Flowering time
Autumn

Pests
Mealybug, scale insects, thrip

PLAYING DEAD
When dormant, button plant can appear to be completely dead. This can be beneficial in its natural habitat, where there are tortoises looking for succulent plants to get moisture from.

Conophytum minutum

HOW TO GROW

In early autumn when temperatures start to cool, water lightly initially, to encourage button plant to break out of dormancy, then increase the water. Once all the leaves are plump, reduce watering until the leaves show a loss in turgidity; ensure the compost dries out completely before rewatering. Feed once or twice early in the growing season with a half-strength, low-nitrogen fertilizer. Button plant does not need to be repotted frequently. When the plant starts to form a large clump, propagate by stem cuttings in autumn, after dormancy has ended (see page 37), or sow seed in autumn (see page 34).

GROWING TIP

If growing button plant indoors, you may need supplementary light from an LED grow lamp during the growing season.

OTHER NOTABLE SPECIES

- *C. calculus* develops large, grey, rounded, fused leaf pairs.
- *C. obcordellum* has uniquely patterned leaves.

Coquimbano

Copiapoa coquimbana

Slow-growing, densely spined coquimbano has globular green stems, 10cm/4in in diameter, which develop offsets from the base and eventually form an impressive mound. The apex of each head is tufted with white hairs, from which yellow flowers appear in summer. It grows in sandy soils in the extremely arid Atacama desert.

—

WHERE TO GROW

Plant coquimbano in a very free-draining mineral soil mix such as one part sharp sand, one part 3–4mm/$^1/_8$–$^1/_6$in potting grit and one part soil-based potting compost, in a shallow pot with good drainage. Place in full sun, although some protection from direct sun in midsummer may be needed. Grow in a cool greenhouse and protect from excessive rain if moved outdoors in summer, ensuring the cactus benefits from good airflow.

—

HOW TO GROW

Coquimbano has adapted to surviving very arid conditions. Water cautiously in spring and summer, with frequent light watering and a deeper water monthly. Reduce water in autumn, and in winter keep the compost completely dry. Feed with high-potassium fertilizer monthly in spring. Pot on as needed into slightly wider pots. This species can be grown from offsets, if available (see Division, page 39). Otherwise sow seed (see page 34). Plants are often grafted (see page 39) to increase their rate of growth.

—

GROWING TIP

Too much water in summer can cause coquimbano to split, producing irreversible scars. If your plant looks overly plump, stop watering to avoid this happening.

ANOTHER NOTABLE SPECIES

• *C. cinerea* is a mostly solitary species with a grey body and contrasting black spines.

Family	Cactaceae
Height and spread	60x100cm/24x39in
Temperature	10–30°C/50–86°F
Position	Bright light
Flowering time	Summer
Pests	Mealybug, red spider mite

DESERT LIFELINE
The flora in the Atacama desert is reliant on regular, dense coastal fogs, which provide the moisture lifeline that keeps these plants alive in between the infrequent rains.

Elephant's tooth cactus

Coryphantha elephantidens

Elephant's tooth cactus is a large globular species that forms multi-headed clumps over time. Its large pronounced tubercles have distinctive recurved spines, and its fragrant flowers are pink or yellow. This species is native to Mexico, where it grows in grasslands and arid scrub.

—

WHERE TO GROW

Grow this species in a frost-free greenhouse or on a bright windowsill in a well-drained mix of one part soil-based potting compost, one part sharp sand, one part potting grit and one part fine pumice. The grit and pumice are needed as its thick taproot is susceptible to rotting (see page 141). Elephant's tooth cactus can tolerate temperatures as low as –3°C/27°F in winter, provided the compost is completely dry, although it is probably best to keep it above freezing.

—

HOW TO GROW

Start to water cautiously in spring and increase it in summer, allowing the compost to dry out thoroughly before watering again. Feed with half-strength fertilizer once or twice in spring; do not overfeed this species. Stop watering in autumn and keep dry in winter. Repot when your plant has outgrown its container. Choose a pot only slightly bigger than the previous one, as overpotting can lead to the compost staying wet for too long. Propagate by removing offsets (see Division, page 39).

—

GROWING TIP

When repotting this cactus, be cautious not to damage the thick taproot.

NOTABLE CULTIVAR

- *C. elephantidens* 'Tanshi Zougemaru Inermis' makes a good child- and pet-friendly cactus because it is spineless.

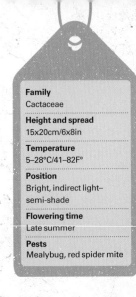

Family	Cactaceae
Height and spread	15x20cm/6x8in
Temperature	5–28°C/41–82F°
Position	Bright, indirect light–semi-shade
Flowering time	Late summer
Pests	Mealybug, red spider mite

AN ELEPHANT TOOTH?
The species name *elephantidens* is derived from Latin and means 'elephant tusk', in reference to the tooth-like spines.

Bear paws

Cotyledon tomentosa subsp. *tomentosa*

This charming, evergreen succulent shrub gets its name from its hairy, paw-shaped leaves with their claw-like appendages. It forms a neat bush and has orange-red, bell-shaped flowers in summer. Bear paws grows on dry rocky slopes in ravine habitats in South Africa.

WHERE TO GROW

Bear paws is perfect for planting in a decorative terracotta pot. Use a free-draining, sandy mix such as one part sharp sand, one part 3–4mm/^{1}/8–^{1}/6in potting grit, one part soil-based potting compost and one part composted bark. Position in a conservatory or on a bright windowsill. It can be moved outdoors in summer; although it tolerates light frosts, bring it indoors before winter.

HOW TO GROW

Water regularly from spring to autumn, allowing the soil to dry out before rewatering. During the hottest periods of summer, the growth of bear paws tends to slow down and go into resting mode, so water sparingly during this time. In winter, water only if the plant is showing signs of stress. Feed with a half-strength balanced fertilizer once a month in the growing season. Propagate from stem cuttings (see page 37) or from seed (see page 34).

GROWING TIP

Light pruning can help to keep a neat shape, and the clippings can be used to grow more plants.

ANOTHER NOTABLE SPECIES

- *C. pendens* is a cliff-dwelling species with a dangling habit, which makes it ideal for a hanging basket (see page 58) or green wall (see page 70).

Family	Crassulaceae
Height and spread	30x30cm/12x12in
Temperature	5–28°C/41–82°F
Position	Bright, indirect light
Flowering time	Summer
Pests	Aphid, mealybug

ATTRACTIVE FLOWERS
The orange-red or yellow, bell-shaped flowers of bear paws are favoured by sunbirds – one of this species' main pollinators.

Green wall

Being well adapted to surviving seemingly inhospitable places, succulents can be found growing in the cracks and crevices of often-vertical cliffs, where they generally thrive. Such cliff-dwelling plants are known as cremnophytes, and it's their ability to survive adversity that makes some of them perfect candidates for a green (or living) wall. In recent years, such walls have become popular as a way of greening our cities. These vertical gardens not only establish a pleasant environment, but can also – if done well – be works of art.

There are many different ways to create a green wall. You could plant a few succulents in the crevasses of a stone wall, or else grow them in a few clay pots attached to a wall; more elaborate systems might clad entire buildings. This project uses an old picture frame, which has been adapted to produce a succulent work of art that can bring a bit of greenery to a sunny wall.

When planting a green wall, it is important to consider the location and select the right species to cope with the local conditions. Also, think about how much light each plant will receive and, if the wall is outdoors, whether it will cope in winter. Select species that have similar watering requirements. Slower-growing and smaller species are often a good choice, especially for small green walls. Consider the weight of the potting medium you use; adding perlite, for example, can help keep your frame lighter.

When your green wall needs some water, remove it from its hanging position and place it horizontally; then water from above. Allow any excess water to drain before hanging it up again.

YOU WILL NEED

- Wooden picture frame, 23x28cm/9x11in
- Plastic mesh, 22x26.5cm/9x10½in
- Staple gun
- 2 pieces, 22cm/9in long, of sawn timber, 5cm/2in wide by 1cm/½in thick
- 2 pieces, 24cm/9½in long, of sawn timber, 5cm/2in wide by 1cm/½in thick
- Panel pin nails, 20mm/¾in long, and hammer
- Wood glue
- Clear wood waterproofing sealant and paintbrush
- 4 screws, 20mm/¾in long, and screwdriver
- Polycarbonate sheet or similar, 22x26.5cm/9x10½in, for the backing piece
- Trowel
- Scissors or wire cutters

1. Attach the plastic mesh to the back of the wooden picture frame with a staple gun.
2. Create a wooden box to fix behind the frame, by fixing the timber pieces together with panel pin nails and wood glue.
3. Waterproof the box and screw the box to the frame. Then attach the backing piece to the box with a staple gun. Make a few holes in the backing piece to allow for excess water to drain away.
4. Fill the box with a soilless, free-draining succulent potting compost.
5. Insert the succulents by cutting a small hole through the mesh into the soil for each one. Leave your planted-up frame horizontal. Water a day or two later.
6. Leave the frame for a few weeks, to ensure all your plants have rooted. Then hang the frame on a sunny wall.

PLANTS USED

Cotyledon pendens, Crassula perforata, Echeveria compressicaulis, E. derenbergii, E. minima, Graptopetalum amethystinum, G. paraguayense, Haworthia turgida, Mammillaria surculosa, Rebutia fabrisii, Sedum adolphi, S. clavatum, S. dasyphyllum, S. × rubrotinctum

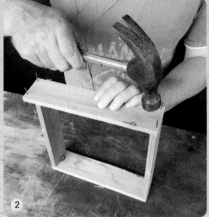

Money plant

Crassula ovata aka Jade plant

Money plant is a popular succulent that grows like a miniature tree with a thick trunk that becomes woody with age (see Succulent bonsai, page 44). It has pinkish white flowers and is very tolerant and easy to care for, making it a good plant for first-time succulent growers. Money plant grows naturally on rocky hillsides on the east coast of southern Africa.

WHERE TO GROW

Plant in a mix of four parts multipurpose potting compost, one part sand and one part potting grit. Place indoors or in a greenhouse or conservatory. Money plant copes well in lower light levels, but does best in a bright location. It can be taken outdoors in summer; move it indoors before winter as it will not tolerate frost.

HOW TO GROW

Water regularly in spring and summer, ensuring the potting compost dries out before watering again. In autumn and winter, water only if the plant starts to look dehydrated. In summer, feed every other week with a half-strength balanced fertilizer. Propagate from stem cuttings (see page 37).

GROWING TIP

When grown indoors, spray the foliage occasionally, to remove any settled dust. Leaves may develop white spots. These are mineral deposits secreted through hydathodes (specialized pores) in the leaves; often mistaken as pests, they are nothing to worry about.

OTHER NOTABLE SPECIES

- *C. arborescens* is a similar species to *C. ovata* but has silver leaves.
- *C. ovata* 'Gollum' has tubular, ear-like leaves.

Family	
Crassulaceae	
Height and spread	
2x1m/7x3ft	
Temperature	
10–28°C/50–82°F	
Position	
Bright, indirect light–semi-shade	
Flowering time	
Spring–summer	
Pests	
Mealybug, red spider mite, scale insect	

MONEY DOESN'T GROW ON TREES
The money plant is said to bring good fortune and prosperity, so is often given as a gift.

Prickle plant

Delosperma echinatum

Prickle plant is a small, slow-growing shrubby succulent native to the Eastern Cape in South Africa, where it inhabits rocky areas of coastal thicket. The leaves, as its species name alludes to, are covered with prickly white hairs. Although the pale yellow flowers are not the showiest compared to others in the genus, prickle plant is definitely worth growing just for its peculiar leaves.

WHERE TO GROW

This species makes a great pot plant in a conservatory or on a bright windowsill, and is a good ground-cover plant in climates that don't receive frost. Plant in a soil-based potting compost with sharp sand, potting grit and sifted compost in equal parts. It prefers bright light and tolerates semi-shade although it will not flower as freely in lower light conditions. Bring indoors in winter, to protect prickle plant from rain and frost.

HOW TO GROW

Keep plants on the dry side in winter. Increase watering from spring to late summer, and reduce it in autumn. Feed monthly with a half-strength balanced fertilizer in the growing season. Propagate by seed (see page 34) or by stem cuttings, 4–6cm/1½–2½in long (see page 37).

GROWING TIP

Prune lightly to keep prickle plant compact.

ANOTHER NOTABLE SPECIES AND GENUS

- *D. cooperi* is a bit more cold tolerant than *D. echinatum*, and can survive light frosts.
- *Lampranthus aureus* puts on quite a show when in full bloom, when it is completely covered with bright orange flowers.

Family	
Aizoaceae	
Height and spread	
20x20cm/8x8in	
Temperature	
5–28°C/41–82°F	
Position	
Bright light	
Flowering time	
Summer	
Pests	
Mealybug, slug, thrip	

WAITING FOR RAIN
Mature seed capsules of Aizoaceae are dry, but hygroscopic (water-absorbing). If there is enough moisture for germation, they absorb water from tha air, open and disperse the seeds.

Painted lady

Echeveria derenbergii aka Mexican rock rose

Fast-growing painted lady occurs naturally
only in Mexico, where it quickly forms a cluster
with multiple offsets. Its orange-yellow flowers
are borne on short stalks from late winter into
spring – big clumps can provide a nice display
of colour. When not in flower, the grey leaves
develop compact rosettes, 5–8cm/2–3¼in across,
with the tips blushing red in summer sun.

—

WHERE TO GROW

Plant in a free-draining potting mix such as one
part potting grit and one part soil-based potting
compost. Although tolerant of light frost if
conditions are dry, it is best to keep painted lady
under cover in colder climates: for example, in
a frost-free greenhouse, a conservatory or on a
bright windowsill or green wall (see page 70).
In warmer climates, plant in a rock garden
(see page 88). In summer, move painted lady
outdoors, if possible. This species can quickly
etiolate in poor light. See also What is a planter?,
page 120.

—

HOW TO GROW

Be careful not to get water in the rosettes. Water
weekly in spring and summer, reduce water in
autumn and give only light, irregular watering
in winter. Feed monthly with a half-strength
balanced fertilizer in the growing season.
Propagate by stem cuttings (see page 37), leaf
cuttings (see page 38) or seed (see page 34).

GROWING TIP

Once an older plant gets tall and leggy, cut off
the top so the mother plant is compact again;
then root the cutting. Removing the older dry
leaves from the plant not only makes the plant
look more appealing, but also to helps prevent
pests and disease.

Family	Crassulaceae
Height and spread	10cmx3m/4inx10ft
Temperature	−1–28°C/30–82°F
Position	Full sun–semi-shade
Flowering time	Late winter–spring
Pests	Mealybug, vine weevil

ANY SUNSCREEN?
Some species of *Echeveria*
produce a white powdery
substance on their leaves to help
protect them from sun. Avoid
touching it as your fingers will
rub off this bloom.

OTHER NOTABLE SPECIES
- *E. affinis* produces almost black leaves.
- *E. agavoides* is a robust species with thick pointed leaves, resembling a small *Agave*.
- *E. purpusiorum* is a slow-growing, often solitary species with red-marked, dark green leaves.

Strawberry cactus

Echinocereus brandegeei

Echinocereus is a genus of very showy plants that produce vibrant red or pink flowers, in early spring; those of strawberry cactus can be orange, pink or red. This quick-growing species can form prostrate clumps of ribbed spiny stems and is native to Mexico, where it grows in desert scrub on exposed rocky hill slopes.

—

WHERE TO GROW

Plant in a free-draining cactus mix of one part soil-based potting compost, one part sand, one part potting grit and one part pumice. As strawberry cactus is fast-growing, use a slightly bigger than normal pot, so it has space to grow. This species prefers a bright location to flower well. Place in a frost-free greenhouse in winter, even though it can tolerate temperatures below freezing if kept completely dry. In spring, move outdoors for better airflow, and protect from the full sun in midsummer.

—

HOW TO GROW

Strawberry cactus is very susceptible to rotting (see page 141) especially in winter, when it should be kept dry. In spring and summer, water regularly allowing the compost time to dry out before rewatering, and reduce watering in autumn. Feed monthly with a high-potassium fertilizer in spring and summer. Repot every 2–3 years or when strawberry cactus has outgrown its pot. Propagate by stem cuttings (see page 37) or by seed sown when temperatures are above 20°C/68°F (see page 34).

—

GROWING TIP

Ensure strawberry cactus has a cool dry winter, to encourage flowering in spring.

ANOTHER NOTABLE SPECIES

- *E. rigidissimus* (rainbow cactus) is solitary or slowly offsetting; its multicoloured spines explain its common name.

Family
Cactaceae
Height and spread
20x50cm/8x20in
Temperature
−12°C/53°F if dry; otherwise 5–28°C/41–82°F
Position
Bright light
Flowering time
Early spring
Pests
Mealybug, red spider mite, scale insect

IT'S A SPINY CANDLE
Echino- is derived from a Greek word meaning 'spiny' or 'prickly' and *cereus* is Latin for 'waxy' or 'candle'.

Sea urchin

Echinopsis ancistrophora aka *E. subdenudata*, Easter lily cactus

Sea urchin is an almost spineless species with a rounded, ribbed body. Multiple smaller heads develop around the plant base, eventually forming clumps. In summer, it produces wonderful, white, tubular, fragrant flowers, to 20cm/8in long, which start to open in the morning and fade by midday the following day. Sea urchin grows in Bolivia on rocky mountain slopes between 600m/2,000ft and 2,500m/8,200ft above sea level.

—

WHERE TO GROW

This species is cold tolerant down to −7°C/19°F if kept dry; however, it is best kept in a greenhouse from autumn to the end of winter. Move outside for spring and summer. It is just as happy on a bright windowsill indoors, but be careful that the plant doesn't get too much direct sunlight in summer. Grow in a shallow pot filled with a free-draining potting compost.

—

Family
Cactaceae

Height and spread
7x10cm/3x4in

Temperature
5–28°C/41–82°F

Position
Bright, indirect light–semi-shade

Flowering time
Summer

Pests
Mealybug, red spider mite, scale insect

WHERE ARE YOU FROM?

A common misconception is that cacti grow in the desert and, although this is true for some, not all of them do. Sea urchin is a good example of a cactus naturally growing in mountainous grassland and woodland regions.

HOW TO GROW

Water from spring to late summer, allowing the compost to dry out fully before watering again, to prevent the roots rotting (see page 141). Slow down watering in autumn and keep the compost dry in winter. Feed in summer with a low-nitrogen but high-phosphorous fertilizer. Repot in spring if sea urchin outgrows its container; otherwise, do this every 3–5 years. After repotting, don't water the plant for a week. Propagate by division of offsets (see page 39) or by seed (see page 34).

—

GROWING TIP

Place sea urchin in a cool spot in winter, away from radiators.

Echinopsis pentlandii

ANOTHER NOTABLE SPECIES
- *E. oxygona* bears a few more spines than sea urchin, and produces an abundance of pale pink, tubular flowers.

Echinopsis oxygona

Echinopsis spiniflora

Grafting cacti

There are many benefits to grafting cacti, including for attaching difficult species on to hardier rootstocks to make them easier to care for or to increase the growth rate of slower-growing species. Grafted plants will typically flower sooner than plants growing on their own roots. In the case of red- and yellow-coloured cacti, grafting is essential for their survival, as these plants typically lack chlorophyll and rely entirely on the green rootstock to photosynthesize. This propagation technique is also a great way of trying to save a plant that has suffered from root rot (see page 141).

Grafting is best done in late spring and summer, when both the rootstock and mother plant are in active growth. Such a technique may sound challenging, but with a bit of practice successful grafting can be easily achieved. Using a small piece of tissue paper helps prevent the sticky tape from damaging the spines and allows for easier removal later on.

SUITABLE SUCCULENTS FOR ROOTSTOCK

Cereus repandus
Echinopsis spachiana
Leucostele chiloensis
Myrtillocactus geometrizans
Selenicereus undatus
Trichocereus macrogonus var. *macrogonus*

1. Sterilize the cutting surface and all tools with disinfectant spray.
2. Remove some of the spines from the rootstock, with snips or a scalpel.
3. Cut through the rootstock (here, *Leucostele chiloensis*) with a knife or scalpel.
4. Bevel the edge at a 45-degree angle.
5. Cut a thin slither through the top of the rootstock, ensuring its top is flat, and leave it on top of the stock.
6. Remove a piece of the cactus you want to graft – the scion – from the mother plant (here, *Tephrocactus bonnieae*) and make a fresh clean cut along the base.
7. Then remove the slither from the rootstock and place the freshly cut scion on top of the stock, ensuring the central vascular rings overlap.
8. Apply gentle downward pressure and wriggle the scion to remove any trapped air bubbles. Place a small piece of tissue paper on the top.
9. Carefully place two or three pieces of clear tape over the scion and stick to the side of the pot. Label and water the grafted plant and place it out of direct sunlight. After a week or so, the graft should fuse, and the tape can be carefully removed.

Peanut cactus

Echinopsis chamaecereus aka *Chamaecereus silvestrii*

This small, low-growing species has narrow trailing stems that start out as small, erect fingers before becoming more prostrate and eventually reaching 15cm/6in long. Older plants form small mats of tangled stems over 30cm/12in across, with bright red flowers. This native of Argentina is thought to grow in mountains between Tucumán and Salta.

—

WHERE TO GROW

Plant peanut cactus in a mix of equal parts soil-based potting compost and potting grit. It is cold tolerant down to −5°C/23°F, if kept dry, but is best grown in a frost-free greenhouse or indoors in a small, shallow pot near a bright window or in a small hanging basket (see page 58). In summer, move it outdoors, so it can benefit from airflow.

—

HOW TO GROW

Keep dry in winter; then from spring to autumn, water regularly but ensure the potting mix is given a chance to dry between waterings. Feed monthly in summer with a half-strength, low-nitrogen fertilizer. Repotting, especially larger plants, can be difficult as the stems tend to break into smaller pieces. Propagate from stem cuttings (see page 37).

—

GROWING TIP

When growing peanut cactus indoors, give it a cool winter-rest period, to encourage flowers from late spring to summer.

Family	
Cactaceae	
Height and spread	
10x30cm/4x12in	
Temperature	
−5°C/23°F if dry; otherwise 5–28°C/41–82°F	
Position	
Bright, indirect light	
Flowering time	
Late spring–summer	
Pests	
Mealybug, red spider mite, scale insect	

LOST BUT NOT GONE
The peanut cactus has not been seen in the wild since it was first collected by Carlo Luigi Spegazzini in 1896.

Orchid cactus

Epiphyllum oxypetalum

Native to tropical regions of South America is the orchid cactus, which grows in trees as an epiphyte. Its flattened fleshy stems are very leaf-like and function in much the same way as a traditional leaf. In summer, large, fragrant, eye-catching, white flowers, to 20cm/8in across, start to open in the afternoon for their bat pollinators, and they close by dawn. A pollinated bloom matures into a bright pink fruit with white flesh pitted with small black seeds.

WHERE TO GROW

Plant in well-draining orchid compost in a hanging basket (see page 58), so the leaf-like stems can hang over the sides. This species does not require a large amount of pot space and can even do well when pot-bound. It is adapted to shady jungles so in summer grow it outdoors in a shady spot. At other times of the year, position it indoors or in a conservatory, ideally not below 10°C/50°F.

Family	
Cactaceae	
Height and spread	
2x1m/7x3ft	
Temperature	
10–28°C/50–82°F	
Position	
Bright, indirect light	
Flowering time	
Late spring–summer	
Pests	
Aphid, mealybug, red spider mite	

LEAF OR STEM?
Early botanists thought that the flowers of this genus were borne by the leaves, so called the genus *Epiphyllum* – the Greek words *epi* and *phyllon* when combined mean 'on the leaf'. However, the leaf-like structures are actually flattened stems known as cladodes.

HOW TO GROW

Use filtered or deionized water to avoid calcium deposits on your plant. Water well and regularly in spring and summer, allowing the compost to almost dry out before watering again. Do not let orchid cactus become too wet or it may rot (see page 141). Reduce watering in autumn and keep dry in winter. Regularly mist in the growing season, and also feed monthly with a balanced fertilizer or foliar feed. Orchid cactus can grow quickly so an occasional light pruning will keep it in shape. Propagate from stem cuttings, 10–15cm/4–6in long (see page 37).

—

GROWING TIP

To encourage flowering, grow orchid cactus in indirect light, keep it a little pot-bound and ensure it has a cool, dry winter rest.

Epiphyllum crenatum var. *chichicastenango*

OTHER NOTABLE SPECIES AND CULTIVARS

- *E. anguliger* (fishbone cactus) has fishbone-like stems.
- *Epiphyllum* cultivars with spectacular flower colours include red-bloomed 'Beautiful Red', pink 'Ophelia', yellow 'Desert Falcon' and orange 'Dragon Heart'.

African milk barrel

Euphorbia polygona var. *horrida*

African milk barrel is a clump-forming stem succulent native to South Africa, with grey-green stems covered in reddish brown thorns. Flowers form in summer at the tip of each stem. Over time and when allowed the room to grow, this species can form impressive mounds.

Family	Euphorbiaceae
Height and spread	1x1m/3x3ft
Temperature	5–28°C/41–82°F
Position	Bright light–indirect light
Flowering time	Summer
Pests	Mealybug (occasionally)

WHERE TO GROW

Grow in a mix of two parts multipurpose soil-based potting compost and one potting grit. Select a pot that is only just large enough for the number of roots. Plant larger plants in shallow pots, to avoid root rot (see page 141). Give small plants bright light, but not direct sunlight as they can scorch, while older plants can tolerate higher light levels. Position in a conservatory or greenhouse; smaller plants also do well on a bright windowsill. Put African milk barrel outdoors in the growing season and then bring indoors before winter.

HOW TO GROW

Start watering lightly in spring and more regularly in summer and give two or three applications of low-nitrogen fertilizer. Reduce water in autumn and stop watering in winter. Propagate by stem cuttings (see page 37). Cut the stem at a joint where possible to minimize the size of the wound. The cut surfaces will produce white latex, which can be an irritant, so take precautions not to get it on your skin. After removing the cut stem, hold it under running water until the latex flow has stopped and then put it in a cool, dry place to callus.

GROWING TIP

The seed pods of *Euphorbia* are explosive capsules. If you want to collect seeds from your plant, cover each seed pod with a mesh bag to catch its seeds when they are ripe.

A PERFECT HOST
In its native habitats, the African milk barrel can be a host to the parasitic mistletoe *Viscum minimum*.

Euphorbia polygona var. *horrida*

Euphorbia meloformis

Euphorbia obesa

NOTABLE CULTIVAR AND ANOTHER NOTABLE SPECIES

- *E. meloformis* produces rounded heads and has a more compact habit (see also South African mini-desert, page 106).
- *E. polygona* var. *horrida* 'Snowflake' is a particularly white-stemmed cultivar.

African milk tree

Euphorbia trigona

The African milk tree is a fast-growing, triangular-stemmed succulent from Angola and central Africa. It forms a multi-branched, upright plant, which can grow up to 3m/10ft, but is unlikely to reach this size as a potted plant. It provides a very architectural focus in a decorative planter.

—

WHERE TO GROW

The ideal placement is near a bright window or in a conservatory. In summer, move African milk tree outdoors, but bring it back indoors before frosts occur. Plant in a mix of two parts soil-based potting compost and one part potting grit.

—

HOW TO GROW

This species needs minimal maintenance and is hassle-free. Water well in spring and summer, allowing the soil to dry out between waterings. In autumn and winter, keep watering to a minimum. In summer, feed with a low-nitrogen fertilizer monthly. Prune large plants to reduce their size if they are getting too big but be cautious of the white latex, which can cause skin irritation. Propagate from stem cuttings (see page 37). After removing the stem, hold the cut end of the stem under running water until the latex flow has completely stopped.

—

GROWING TIP

During periods of drought, this species tends to drop its leaves. To avoid leaf drops, do not leave the soil too dry for extended periods of time during warm periods.

Family
Euphorbiaceae

Height and spread
1–2mx0.5m/3–7x1½ft

Temperature
1–28°C/34–82°F

Position
Bright, indirect light

Flowering time
Summer

Pests
Mealybug (occasionally)

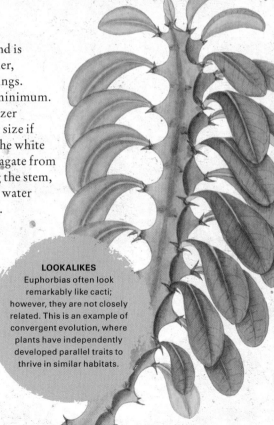

LOOKALIKES
Euphorbias often look remarkably like cacti; however, they are not closely related. This is an example of convergent evolution, where plants have independently developed parallel traits to thrive in similar habitats.

OTHER NOTABLE SPECIES

- *E. globosa* has rounded stem segments.
- *E. lactea* develops whitish, ghost-like stems.

Tiger jaws

Faucaria tuberculosa

This low-growing, clump-forming succulent produces triangular, green-grey leaves, the margins and upper surfaces of which bear white tubercles. It is these toothlike appendages that give tiger jaws its common name. It bears abundant, bright yellow flowers, 4cm/1½in across, which close at night, only to open again by midday the following day; on cloudy days, they may not open at all, to protect its precious, delicate flowers while pollinators are not out and about. Tiger jaws grows in rocky habitats in the thickets of the Eastern Cape, South Africa.

—

WHERE TO GROW

This species is an easy plant to grow on a windowsill or in a greenhouse and may also do well in a protected spot in a rock garden (see page 88). If the plant gets too much sun in midsummer, its leaves turn red, to shield it from sunburn. In winter, protect it from cold wet weather. Plant in a sandy potting mix with low organic matter, such as one part sharp sand, one part potting grit and one part sifted composted bark.

—

Family
Aizoaceae
Height and spread
5x15cm/2x6in
Temperature
5–28°C/41–82°F
Position
Bright light–semi-shade
Flowering time
Late summer–autumn
Pests
Mealybug

TEETH WITH A PURPOSE
The toothlike appendages on tiger jaws are great at catching moisture from mist and fog. The droplets are then directed to the roots.

HOW TO GROW

Water well in spring and autumn; ensure the compost dries out completely before watering again. In midsummer, tiger jaws can go into a rest phase and needs less water. In winter, keep the compost dry; give only the occasional drop of water if your plant looks dehydrated. Remove some of the older leaves and feed monthly with a half-strength fertilizer through the growing season. Repot every three years. Propagate from seed (see page 34) or stem cuttings (see page 37).

GROWING TIP

After five years of growth, plants can become a bit woody and are susceptible to losing their roots, so take cuttings before they reach this stage.

ANOTHER NOTABLE SPECIES

- *F. felina* has white flowers.

Rock garden

A rock or crevice garden is a fantastic place to grow and display succulents; after all, many species can be found growing naturally among rocky outcrops. Rock gardening is not something new – we have been building such gardens in one form or another for thousands of years, from the early Japanese stone gardens or, arguably, even from the stone monuments such as Stonehenge. The first modern-day rock gardens appeared in the mid-1800s after botanists had returned with 'strange' plants from mountainous regions, and dedicated rock gardens for growing alpine plants started appearing throughout Europe. However, probably the first rock garden to grow these plants in the UK was constructed at Chelsea Physic Garden, in London, in 1774; another old one and one of the largest rock gardens in the world was started at the Royal Botanic Gardens, Kew, also in London, in 1882. The garden holds over 3,000 different species. One of the first rock gardens to appear in America was built at Brooklyn Botanic Garden in 1917, while huge earthworks were involved in the construction of the rock garden at Utrecht University Botanic Gardens in 1963, for which 2,100 tonnes of rock were imported from the Ardennes.

A rock garden can comprise some well-placed, large boulders in a sunny part of your garden or, more simply, some strategically placed rocks in a stone trough or small clay pot. When planning your rock garden, consider your climate and ensure all the species you choose can tolerate being grown outdoors in your area. Alternatively, you could create a smaller garden, which can be brought indoors in winter. Get some inspiration from nature, gather pictures of plants growing in rocky outcrops or plan a trip to see them in their habitats.

PLANTS USED

Crassula brevifolia, C. rupestris
Echeveria compressicaulis
Fenestraria rhopalophylla
Graptopetalum pachyphyllum
Haworthia monticola
Sedum clavatum

1. Place a layer of drainage material such as pumice on the bottom of a large container.
2. Add a thick layer of horticultural sharp sand to within 5cm/2in of the container rim.
3. Choose a selection of rocks that are of the same type, so they look as if they come from the same outcrop. Bury about one-third of each rock into the sand, creating height and level changes as well as an iceberg effect in which it appears that there is much more of the rock below the ground.
4. Fill in the gaps with a sandy, free-draining potting mix.
5. Plant your succulents into the cracks and crevices between the rocks.
6. Topdress with a decorative sand or gravel that complements the rocks.
7. Leave the rock garden for a day or two; then water it.

Baby's toes

Fenestraria rhopalophylla

In its natural sandy environment in Namibia and South Africa, the leaves of baby's toes are almost completely submerged – only the translucent tips are exposed. These enable light to penetrate chlorophyll in the leaves hidden beneath the sand. The flowers are white or yellow.

—

WHERE TO GROW

Plant in a shallow container with a free-draining sandy potting mix with very little to no organic material: for example, use a mix of two parts sharp sand, one part soil-based potting compost, one part potting grit and one part sifted composted bark. Position on a sunny windowsill or in a conservatory, greenhouse or rock garden (see page 88). See also South African mini-desert, page 106.

—

HOW TO GROW

Water sparingly from spring to autumn, reducing water during the hottest summer periods. Wait for the leaves to become slightly less turgid before giving your plant another drink. Too much water will cause its leaves to grow proud of the soil; by ensuring the compost dries out between watering, the resultant growth will be compact and low above the soil. Do not water in winter. Give a half-strength, low-nitrogen feed monthly in spring. Repot every 3–5 years in the growing season. Propagate by dividing clumps (see page 39).

—

GROWING TIP

When repotting it, plant baby's toes sufficiently deep that only the leaf tips show. A topdressing of coarse silica sand gives a natural look.

NOTABLE SUBSPECIES

- *F. rhopalophylla* subsp. *aurantiaca* is a yellow-flowered subspecies from Northern Cape in South Africa and Namibia.
- *F. rhopalophylla* subsp. *rhopalophylla* has white flowers and is endemic to Namibia.

Family
Aizoaceae
Height and spread
5x10–30cm/2x4–12in
Temperature
5–28°C/41–82°F
Position
Bright light
Flowering time
Late summer–autumn
Pests
Mealybug, thrip

HIDDEN BENEATH THE SAND
Being mostly submerged is a great way for a plant to conserve water and hide away from thirsty tortoises.

Devil's tongue barrel cactus

Ferocactus latispinus

This single-headed cactus, over time, forms a ribbed, rounded, green body covered with red radial spines, where the central spine is larger and flattened with a hooked tip – giving this species its common name. Purple-mauve or occasionally yellow flowers, to 6cm/2½in long, appear in clusters around the apex of devil's tongue barrel cactus, which grows in dry grassland and rocky scrub in central and southern Mexico.

—

WHERE TO GROW

Grow in a decorative pot in a free-draining cactus mix such as one part soil-based potting compost, one part sharp sand and one part potting grit. Do not overpot. This species does well in a greenhouse and on a bright windowsill. In summer, move it outdoors, but avoid direct sunlight in midsummer as devil's tongue barrel cactus can suffer from scorch

—

Family
Cactaceae

Height and spread
30x30cm/12x12in

Temperature
5–28°C/5–82°F

Position
Bright, indirect light

Flowering time
Late autumn–early winter

Pests
Mealybug, red spider mite, scale insect

MUTUALLY BENEFICIAL
Ferocactus has extrafloral nectaries embedded in each areole at the bases of the spines. This provides a nectar reward for ants, which in return help protect the plant from herbivores.

HOW TO GROW

Start watering from spring, lightly to start with and then increase watering in the growing season. Ensure that the substrate has sufficient time to dry out before rewatering. Slow down watering in autumn, watering only during bright weather, and keep completely dry in winter. Feed with a low-nitrogen fertilizer monthly in spring and summer. In early spring, repot once devil's tongue barrel cactus has outgrown its pot, or every 3–4 years. Propagate by seed (see page 34).

GROWING TIP

Plant in a shallow pot only a little wider than the body of the plant. As your plant grows, larger terracotta bowls can work well.

Ferocactus glaucescens

OTHER NOTABLE SPECIES

- *F. glaucescens* has a blue-grey body.
- *F. pilosus* produces small, wiry hairs among its sharp spines.

Ferocactus pilosus

Dwarf ox-tongue

Gasteria bicolor var. *liliputana* aka Lilliput gasteria

Dwarf ox-tongue is a small, compact succulent that produces clumps over time. Each tongue-shaped, white-spotted leaf, 1–5cm/½–2in long, has fine, serrated margins and a pointed tip. Orange, balloon-shaped flowers, with green-and-white-tipped petals, are held on a flowering stem. This variety is endemic to the Eastern Cape in South Africa, where it grows on sandstone ridges in Albany thickets.

WHERE TO GROW

Grow in a shallow pot in a nutrient-poor, free-draining soil mix comprising one part soil-based potting compost, one part potting grit and one part sharp sand. Place on a windowsill, in a conservatory or greenhouse, or outdoors in a pot or rock garden (see page 88). Bring indoors in frosty weather or during extended rainy periods. Its small size and compact habit make dwarf ox-tongue ideal to add to a companion planter.

HOW TO GROW

This plant grows naturally in a winter-rainfall region so, in cultivation, watering should be year-round. However, in midwinter, when day lengths are very short, water lightly and cautiously, avoiding the potting compost staying wet for too long. In summer, especially if planted in full sun, dwarf ox-tongue growth can slow down and go into summer dormancy, where the leaves turn reddish to cope with the intense light and water stress. Repot every 2–3 years; at the same time, remove any dead roots. Propagate by dividing big clumps (see page 39) or by taking leaf cuttings (see page 37).

GROWING TIP

With *Gasteria* less is often more when it comes to watering. This genus can lose its roots easily if overwatered; luckily, it generally recovers, producing new roots with time.

Family	
Asphodelaceae	
Height and spread	
5x25cm/2x10in	
Temperature	
10–28°C/50–82°F	
Position	
Bright, indirect light–semi-shade	
Flowering time	
Winter–early spring	
Pests	
Aphid, mealybug	

WHAT'S IN A NAME?
Gasteria comes from the Greek word meaning stomach, which refers to the swollen base on the flowers. *Liliputana* is derived from the island inhabited by miniature people in *Gulliver's Travels* and reflects the diminutive nature of this succulent.

ANOTHER NOTABLE SPECIES
- *G. acinacifolia* is one of the largest species, with rosettes up to 75cm/30in high and 65cm/26in wide.

Succulent wreath

A succulent wreath is an attractive alternative to a more traditional holly (*Ilex*) or ivy (*Hedera*) wreath, and you need not wait until Christmas to make one. It provides a wow factor, and is surprisingly quick and easy to make. It can be hung on a door or a wall, or used as a creative centrepiece for a table setting. Another good thing about a succulent wreath is that it is living, so with a bit of care it will look great for longer than a holly or ivy wreath.

Because such a wide variety of succulent plants is available, the combinations for your wreath are endless. Grab a range of your favourite succulents, considering their form, colour and how they look in combination, as well as their cultural needs. Use flat moss or sphagnum moss to hold your wreath together, and you can also add Spanish moss (*Tillandsia usneoides*) or reindeer moss (*Cladonia rangiferina*). Pre-formed wire wreaths can be easily purchased and come in a range of sizes.

Water your succulent wreath weekly by soaking it in a shallow tray. In between waterings, give your wreath an occasional misting. Once you have finished with your wreath, the succulents can be removed and potted individually or introduced in other arrangements.

PLANTS USED

Aeonium goochiae 'Ballerina'
Crassula perforata
Echeveria compressicaulis
Graptopetalum amethystinum,
   G. paraguayense
Sedum adolphi, S. clavatum
Tillandsia usneoides

1. Lay a wire wreath on to some flat or sphagnum moss.
2. Place some coco peat on top and cover over with the moss.
3. Wrap the moss wreath with floristry wire, to hold everything together.
4. Trim off any loose moss.
5. Poke holes in the wreath and insert a succulent into each hole; secure with floristry pins.
6. Water your wreath and leave it horizontal in a bright location for a few days to a week, to root in, then hang it on a door or wall.

Ghost plant

Graptopetalum paraguayense

This clump-forming succulent has rosettes of thick grey leaves that make it look like an *Echeveria* (see page 74). Its five-petalled, star-shaped, white flowers form in clusters from early spring.

—

WHERE TO GROW

The ghost plant needs a fair amount of light to stop it from etiolating. If growing it indoors, place in the brightest window you have. It also does well on a green wall (see page 70) and in a succulent wreath (see page 94). Plant in a free-draining potting mix of one part soil-based potting compost, one part sharp sand and one part potting grit.

—

HOW TO GROW

Being very drought hardy, ghost plant can withstand long periods without water. Water more often in spring and summer, ensuring the potting compost has dried out between waterings. Reduce water in autumn and keep the compost bone dry in cold weather and in winter. Feed once or twice in the growing season with a half-strength, low-nitrogen fertilizer. Propagate by stem cuttings, taken 1–2cm/½–¾in below a leaf rosette (see page 37), or by leaf cuttings (see page 38).

—

Family	Crassulaceae
Height and spread	10x15cm/4x6in
Temperature	–5–28°C/23–82°F
Position	Bright light
Flowering time	Early spring
Pests	Mealybug

GROWING TIP
When ghost plant starts to get a bit scraggly, remove some of the heads to keep the habit compact and propagate a new plant.

Graptopetalum bellum

ANOTHER NOTABLE SPECIES
• *G. bellum*, a native of Mexico, produces masses of rose-pink flowers in spring.

THE ILLUSIVE GHOST
Graptopetalum paraguayense was first brought into cultivation as a weed among some cacti imported into New York in 1904. Initially thought to be native to Paraguay, as its name suggests, it is still not known where this species grows naturally, although it is most likely native to an isolated slope somewhere in Mexico.

Giant chin cactus

Gymnocalycium saglionis

The giant chin cactus is a striking, solitary barrel cactus with a flattened top. It is covered with curved, reddish brown or black spines that slowly turn grey with age. The body is blue-green with prominent tubercles, creating an appealing pattern. Its pale pink to white flowers, when flowering well, can produce a floral crown. This species is native to Argentina, where it grows on dry, rocky mountain slopes.

—

WHERE TO GROW

Giant chin cactus makes a fantastic specimen plant in a large terracotta bowl or Wardian case (see page 100) in a free-draining, slightly acidic potting compost (see also What is a planter?, page 120). Growth tends to slow if the compost becomes too alkaline; avoid using tap water, or repot every 2–3 years to avoid this. In frost-free climates, grow it in a rock garden (see page 88). Protect from cold and rain by placing in a bright spot indoors from autumn; take outdoors in summer or keep it in a conservatory or on a bright windowsill. Avoid intense sunlight in midsummer, as this can scorch giant chin cactus.

—

HOW TO GROW

Keep this species dry in winter and start watering with rainwater from spring through to autumn. During active growth, water regularly, allowing the soil to dry out between waterings. Fertilize every month in spring and summer, with a half-strength, low-nitrogen feed. Repot every 2–3 years or when giant chin cactus outgrows its pot. Propagate by seed (see page 34).

—

GROWING TIP

When repotting giant chin cactus, choose a slightly larger, squat pot rather than one that is too deep.

OTHER NOTABLE SPECIES
- *G. amerhauseri* develops spines that are pressed flat against the plant's body.
- *G. horstii* has fewer spines than *G. saglionis*.
- *G. mihanovichii* has colourful markings and is an attractive species.

Family	
Cactaceae	
Height and spread	
90x40cm/36x16in	
Temperature	
0–28°C/32–82°F	
Position	
Bright light	
Flowering time	
Summer	
Pests	
Mealybug, scale insect	

SETTING SEED
When ripe, the fleshy pink fruits split down one side, exposing green, edible pulp pitted with small, black seeds.

Zebra plant

Haworthiopsis fasciata

Zebra plant is a low-growing, clumping plant that eventually forms small mounds of dwarf, aloe-like rosettes. The lower surfaces of its lance-shaped leaves are covered with white tubercles, which create a zebra-like patterning. It also bears spikes of dainty white flowers. This species grows naturally among fynbos and Albany thickets in rocky areas of the Eastern Cape, South Africa.

WHERE TO GROW

Because it has shallow roots, only 5cm/2in long, plant it in a shallow pot in a free-draining potting compost, comprising equal parts soil-based potting compost, sharp sand and potting grit. In its natural habitat, zebra plant is protected from direct sunlight by shrubs or rocks, and it flushes red in colour if it receives too much sunlight. It is not cold tolerant, so keep indoors in winter in a frost-free greenhouse or on a windowsill.

HOW TO GROW

Water regularly in autumn. In winter, reduce watering during periods of low light; increase it again in spring. In summer, water sparingly especially if the plant starts to flush red; the fleshy roots tend to dry in summer and will rot during this time if kept too wet. Repot every 2–3 years; while doing this, remove dead roots and clear dried leaves from the plant base. Propagate by division (see page 39).

GROWING TIP

New roots form from just below the lower leaves. Therefore, when potting, ensure zebra plant is properly bedded into the pot so its roots can find the soil easily.

OTHER NOTABLE SPECIES

- *H. attenuata*, also called zebra plant, has rough upper and lower leaf surfaces, whereas *H. fasciata* has tubercles only on the lower surfaces (see also Recycled pallet planter, page 114).
- *H. limifolia* is a larger plant and suckers a bit more slowly than does *H. fasciata*.

Family
Asphodelaceae

Height and spread
15x30cm/6x12in

Temperature
10–28°C/50–82°F

Position
Bright, indirect light

Flowering time
Spring

Pests
Mealybug

CHARMING PLANT
Local South African folklore suggests that zebra plant can ward off evil spirits.

Wardian case

The Wardian case is probably one of the earliest examples of the modern-day terrarium. In the early nineteenth century, botanists were returning with many botanical marvels from their travels around the world. Unfortunately, many of the plants they collected struggled to survive the long voyage back home, as they were suffering from adverse weather, salt spray, lack of fresh water and poor light levels if kept below deck. The invention of the Wardian case by Dr Nathaniel Bagshaw Ward in 1829 changed this; thereafter, by using such sealed glass crates, botanists were able to successfully transport a diversity of plants around the globe. Sir Joseph Dalton Hooker, director of the Royal Botanic Gardens, Kew, was one of the first explorers to use the Wardian case after plant exploration in New Zealand. These cases also became popular as decorative items, and developed into the modern-day terrarium.

Here, to pay homage to the early explorers, I have recreated a small Wardian case using some small picture frames and filled it with a few of my favourite succulents. All the plants I have selected are either slow growing or stay small so they will not outgrow my Wardian case too quickly.

When planting such a sealed glass container with succulent plants, it's important to remember the Wardian case was designed to keep humidity high, which is not ideal for growing most succulents. For this reason, when choosing one for succulents, find one with a large opening, or vents, which will allow excess humidity to escape. Many will not have any drainage holes either, so it is important to water carefully, so your plants do not quickly succumb to excess moisture. Always place your new creation where the plants will receive ample sunlight.

YOU WILL NEED

- 11 wooden glazed picture frames, 12x17cm/5x7in
- Wood glue
- Electric drill
- Screws and screwdriver
- Nails and hammer
- 3 pieces, 35.5cm/14in long, of sawn timber, 5cm/2in wide by 1cm/½in thick
- 2 pieces, 14cm/5½in long, of sawn timber, 5cm/2in wide by 1cm/½in thick
- 6 brass hinges, 3x3cm/1¼x1¼in
- Pencil
- Glazing putty

1. Remove the backing and glass from each picture frame.
2. Glue a long side of two frames together, then drill a hole and screw together.
3. Glue a third frame to the structure and screw in position. Repeat steps 2 and 3 to make a second three-frame structure.
4. Glue and screw a picture frame at right angles to one of the three-frame structures. Repeat for the second three-frame structure.
5. To make a base for the Wardian case, glue and nail two long pieces to two shorter pieces of sawn timber.
6. On one of the remaining three picture frames, pencil in where two hinges are to be fixed on this piece of the Wardian case lid.
7. Drill and screw in place. Repeat steps 6 and 7 on the other two remaining picture frames.
8. Replace a pane of glass into each picture frame and putty into position.
9. Drill and screw the three lid frames into position on to the remaining long piece of sawn timber.
10. Place a drainage layer of pumice or aggregate at the bottom of the Wardian case and top it with a suitable cactus and succulent potting compost. Plant your succulents (here, *Gymnocalycium* spp., *Astrophytum asterias* 'Super Kabuto' and *Matucana madisoniorum*) and add any rocks or accessories. Top it off with decorative gravel.

Wax plant

Hoya carnosa

This semi-succulent climber has waxy, elliptical leaves. It is native to Australasia, where it grows in subtropical humid forests. Wax plant is a reliable and generally good flowerer, bearing night-scented, star-shaped, red-centred, white or pink blooms in clusters between spring and summer.

—

WHERE TO GROW

This species requires some support or somewhere to climb, so provide a bamboo hoop or trellis. It is also a great choice for a hanging basket (see page 58). Wax plant does well in indirect bright light and tolerates lower light levels, so it is a good house plant. It also does well in a heated conservatory or greenhouse. Plant in a free-draining mix of equal parts multipurpose potting compost, bark and perlite or pumice.

—

Family
Apocynaceae

Height and spread
5x1m/16x3ft

Temperature
10–28°C/50–82°F

Position
Bright, indirect light

Flowering time
Spring–summer

Pests
Mealybug; occasionally red spider mite particularly in drier environments

SPECIALIZED POLLINATION

The night-scented blooms of wax plant attract moths – one of their main pollinators. The blooms have a complex pollination system: when feeding on the nectar, the visiting insect removes the pollinia (a specialized structure holding the pollen). When visiting the next flower, the pollinia is captured by a guide rail on the stigma and is then left behind when the insect flies away.

Hoya erythrina

HOW TO GROW

The wax plant needs more water than most succulents. Water it well from spring to autumn, but be sure the potting medium dries out before rewatering. In winter, reduce watering as growth slows. Feed regularly in summer with a balanced fertilizer. This species can grow fairly quickly so regular light pruning may be needed: at the end of winter, cut back any thin growth and reduce any long stems by one-third. Don't prune flowering stems as they will flower the following year. The wax plant will not respond well to hard pruning. Repot every 2–3 years. Propagate by stem cuttings, 5–6cm/2–2½in long (see page 37).

GROWING TIP

Wax plant comes from areas of high humidity so the foliage needs daily misting. Avoid tap water with a high calcium content as this will leave white deposits on the leaf surfaces. Rainwater, distilled or filtered water is preferable.

OTHER NOTABLE SPECIES
- *H. kerrii* has perfect, heart-shaped leaves and red-centred, white flowers.
- *H. linearis* develops cylindrical, hairy leaves and dainty white flowers.
- *H. pubicalyx* produces vivid red flowers.

Living stones

Lithops pseudotruncatella

The rocky arid regions of Namibia are the native habitat of living stones, which, like other *Lithops*, produces a pair of opposite, succulent leaves sunken below ground level, with only the tops of the leaves showing. The leaves perfectly mimic the surrounding gravel so any passing tortoise does not see them as a tasty treat. In late summer and autumn, this species produces bright yellow flowers, 4cm/1½in across.

WHERE TO GROW

Plant in a sandy mix with minimal organic matter, such as two parts silica or sharp sand, one part potting grit and one part sifted composted bark. Pot in a small shallow container, because living stones has shallow roots. A terracotta pot is ideal. Give it a bright location in a greenhouse or on a sunny windowsill, but avoid direct sunlight in midsummer, when this succulent can scorch.

Family	Aizoaceae
Height and spread	1x2–10cm/½x¾–4in
Temperature	5–28°C/41–82°F
Position	Bright, indirect light
Flowering time	Late summer–autumn
Pests	Mealybug, red spider mite, thrip

WINDOW TO THE BELOW
The window-like, translucent patterns on *Lithops* leaves often lack pigment. Thus, light can penetrate the body of the leaf, where it encounters chlorophyll hidden below ground – in a phenomenon known as fenestration.

Lithops gesineaè

HOW TO GROW

When living stones comes into growth, two new leaves emerge from the centre of the old leaves. During this winter growth phase, do not water, as the plant will recycle the moisture from the old leaves. (If you mistakenly water at this time, the older leaves will be retained and look unnatural.) Once the old leaves have dried, water only when the new leaves feel soft. If you water them too much when firm, they tend to split, leaving scars. Cautious watering will also help to keep your plant from etiolating, especially in winter. Feed once a year in the growing season with a half-strength, low-nitrogen fertilizer. Living stones is slow growing and rarely becomes pot-bound; therefore, repot every 4–5 years. Propagate by seed (see page 34).

GROWING TIP

Light misting once a week in sunny weather keeps living stones cool and helps deter red spider mite (see page 139); it gives the plant a light watering, too.

OTHER NOTABLE SPECIES
- *L. dinteri* has a distinctive brown body and fissured markings.
- *L. hookeri* with its bright yellow flowers is named after the Kew director and botanist Sir Joseph Dalton Hooker.

South African mini-desert

Succulents rarely grow alone in their natural habit but rather in communities, so why not try combining some of your favourite succulents in a shallow planter to make a mini-landscape. Here I have taken a collection of succulents from the deserts of South Africa to make my mini-desert.

A large, shallow terracotta pot or similar is great if you have limited space to grow succulents, and it makes an appealing centrepiece or focal point. You could move your pot outdoors when the season is warm enough and back into a conservatory or greenhouse or into your home near a bright window if the weather is unfavourable.

Choose species that work well together, and think about how they will complement each other with their forms, textures and colours. Resist the temptation to use too many plants; they may look great at first but can quickly become overcrowded as they compete for space. It is also wise to pick plants that don't grow quickly as this will make your planter lower maintenance and increase the longevity of its display.

PLANTS USED
Adromischus sp.
Crassula sericea, C. socialis
Euphorbia meloformis
Fenestraria rhopalophylla
Haworthia sp.
Lithops gesineae
Stapelia sp.
Tylecodon paniculatus

1. Cover each drainage hole with a piece of mesh.
2. Place a layer of aggregate or pumice in the base of the pot.
3. Fill the pot halfway with a free-draining succulent potting compost.
4. Arrange your plants and rocks until you are happy with the composition.
5. Insert the plants, and bed in the rocks so they appear to be emerging out of the ground rather than sitting on top. Then fill in the gaps with more potting compost.
6. Brush off any soil that may have spilt on to the plants and rocks with a small brush.
7. Finish off with a decorative sand or gravel. Brush off any spilt topdressing; then water a day or two later.

Peyote

Lophophora williamsii

Peyote is a small, button-like, grey-green cactus, which is slow growing and usually solitary but with age develops small clusters. It is completely spineless, producing clusters of hairy tufts from the tubercles and the apex. Small pink flowers appear from the centre of the plant, followed by pink fruit reminiscent of tiny chilli peppers. This species is native to Mexico and Texas, USA, where it grows in arid scrub, often among rocks or at the bases of other shrubs. In the dry season, it sinks below the limestone desert sand.

—

WHERE TO GROW

Plant in a pot filled with a very well-drained mineral soil comprising one part soil-based potting compost, one part potting grit, one part sharp sand and one part pumice. Position in a cool greenhouse or on a windowsill; in winter, keep it away from radiators. In summer, move it outdoors and protect from excessive rain.

—

HOW TO GROW

Keep this species dry in autumn and winter. Water cautiously in spring and summer, waiting until the head starts to feel a bit soft before giving it any water, to plump it back up again; it is susceptible to rotting, due to overwatering. Feed once in summer with a low-nitrogen fertilizer. Repot if it has outgrown its pot or every 4–5 years. Propagate by removing offsets by division (see page 39) or by seed (see page 34). Seedlings are slow to establish and are often grafted to speed up their growth (see pages 39 and 78).

—

GROWING TIP

To keep the hairy tufts looking fresh, avoid wetting them. If they do become stale, fluff them up with a toothbrush.

OTHER NOTABLE SPECIES
- *L. diffusa* has white flowers.
- *L. williamsii* var. *caespitosa* bears multiple, small, button-like heads whereas the species is typically solitary.
- *L. williamsii* 'Cristata' develops a strange, brain-like shape.

Family	Cactaceae
Height and spread	3x15cm/1¼x6in
Temperature	5–28°C/41–82°F
Position	Bright, indirect light–semi-shade
Flowering time	Summer
Pests	Mealybug, red spider mite

POTIONS FOR PROTECTION
Peyote contains an alkaloid that protects the plant from herbivores. This alkaloid has been used for shaman rituals and sadly, as a result, wild plants are being overharvested. Plants in cultivation have extremely low concentrations of the alkaloid.

Matucana

Matucana madisoniorum

This Peruvian cactus species is a small, often single-headed, globular plant coloured grey-green. Plants tend to be spineless or have long curved spines, often losing them when older. Older plants produce offsets, but this takes some time as growth can be very slow. Clusters of spectacular, orange, tubular flowers reliably appear from the centre of the plant once it is mature enough – typically 3–5 years from seed. This species grows at low altitudes in subtropical to tropical dry forests.

—

WHERE TO GROW
Matucana does well in bright light, but direct midday sunlight is best avoided. Use a very free-draining potting compost comprising equal parts soil-based potting compost, sharp sand, potting grit or pumice and sifted composted bark. Grow on a bright windowsill, in a Wardian case (see page 100) or in a heated conservatory.

—

HOW TO GROW
Water well in spring and summer, letting the potting compost dry out completely before giving any more water; do not let matucana remain wet for too long. Leave it dry in autumn and winter. Fertilize in summer with a half-strength, low-nitrogen feed. Repot in spring if pot-bound; don't be tempted to increase the pot size too quickly. Red spider mite can cause unsightly and often permanent markings so treat promptly (see page 139). Propagate by seed (see page 34).

—

GROWING TIP
Be careful when you handle matucana, as its spines are very brittle and can easily break off.

ANOTHER NOTABLE SPECIES
• *M. paucicostata* forms a compact cushion of multiple stems.

Family	
Cactaceae	
Height and spread	
15x10cm/6x4in	
Temperature	
10–28°C/50–82°F	
Position	
Bright light–filtered sun	
Flowering time	
Summer	
Pests	
Mealybug, red spider mite, scale insect	

BUYERS BEWARE
This is a very rare species in its natural habitat and is known from only one location. When buying it, be sure that the plant is from cultivated origin and not illegally harvested from the wild.

Blue candle cactus

Myrtillocactus geometrizans aka Bilberry cactus

The blue candle cactus has an arborescent (tree-like) habit and develops multiple, blue-grey, ribbed stems. Flowers are small and white to yellow. It grows naturally in the deserts of Mexico.

—

WHERE TO GROW

Find a sunny spot where blue candle cactus will have room to grow – a conservatory or greenhouse will provide ideal conditions. Move it outdoors in summer, once the temperature stays above 10°C/50°F. Use a well-drained potting compost with little organic matter, such as equal parts soil-based potting compost, potting grit and sharp sand. Place in a pot that allows a bit of room for growth.

—

HOW TO GROW

Water thoroughly in spring and summer, allowing the compost to dry out completely before rewatering. In winter, keep the compost dry. Fertilize with a half-strength balanced fertilizer monthly in summer. Repot every 2–3 years or when the plant outgrows its pot. Propagate from stem cuttings (see page 37). Blue candle cactus also makes a suitable rootstock for grafting (see page 78).

—

GROWING TIP

Don't be tempted to overpot your plant. This could lead to the potting compost staying wet for long periods and may cause root rot (see page 141).

Family
Cactaceae
Height and spread
5x1.5m/16x5ft
Temperature
10–28°C/50–82°F
Position
Bright light
Flowering time
Spring
Pests
Mealybug, red spider mite, scale insect

BERRY PICKING
If you are lucky enough to get fruit forming on your blue candle cactus, you can eat the sweet dark berries, which are similar in appearance to bilberries (*Vaccinium myrtillus*) – hence its botanical name.

NOTABLE CULTIVAR
• 'Fukurokuryuzinboku' (booby cactus) has tubercles that somewhat resemble women's breasts.

Bunny ears cactus

Opuntia microdasys

Native to Mexico is bunny ears cactus, which grows on dry scrubby hillsides in calcareous soil. Its flattened pads (stems) are spineless, but don't be fooled – each areole is a cluster of tiny sharp glochids (barbed bristles). These areoles are reflected in its name *microdasys*, meaning 'small and hairy' in Latin. The new pads can resemble a rabbit's ears, giving this species its common name. Although it can be reluctant to bloom, when this plant does it produces bright yellow, cup-shaped flowers.

Family	Cactaceae
Height and spread	60x45cm/24x18in
Temperature	5–28°C/41–82°F
Position	Bright light
Flowering time	Late spring–summer
Pests	Mealybug, scale insect

WHERE TO GROW

Plant in a well-drained potting mix such as equal parts soil-based potting compost, potting grit and sharp sand. Bunny ears cactus requires lots of light in spring and summer, so it benefits from being moved outdoors from mid-spring. In autumn, bring it back indoors for winter, into a cooler area of your house.

HOW TO GROW

Water regularly in spring and summer, allowing the soil to dry out before rewatering. In autumn, reduce watering, and keep dry in winter or water only lightly if required. Feed monthly with a half-strength, low-nitrogen fertilizer in spring and summer. Occasional light pruning might be needed to keep it in shape; remove a few pads after flowering in summer. Propagate by stem cuttings (see page 37).

NEED A DRINK?
The many glochids covering the pads of bunny ears cactus not only help to protect the plant but are also good at catching moisture from mists and dews.

GROWING TIP

Wear thick gloves when handling bunny ears cactus as its glochids can cause intense irritation to the skin.

OTHER NOTABLE SPECIES
- *O. basilaris* (beaver tail cactus) has bright pink flowers and flushed pink pads.
- *O. microdasys* 'Albata' is covered with white glochids and produces yellow flowers.

Madagascan palm

Pachypodium lamerei

This strange-looking, architectural plant, reminiscent of a
palm tree, makes a fascinating addition to any plant collection.
Its Latin name *Pachypodium* means 'thick foot', because it has
swollen stems, which store water when conditions are harsh.
The thick succulent trunk is covered with thorns, and at the
top of each branch is a cluster of leaves. With age (ten or so
years), this species produces brilliant white, large flowers.

Family	Apocynaceae
Height and spread	3–6mx1–2m/10–20x3–7ft
Temperature	10–28°C/50–82°F
Position	Bright, indirect light
Flowering time	Spring–summer
Pests	Mealybug, red spider mite

WHERE TO GROW

Plant in a very free-draining mix such as one part soil-based
potting compost, one part potting grit, one part sharp sand and
one part sifted composted bark. Ensure the compost dries out
completely before rewatering, to avoid root rot (see page 141).
Do not overpot Madagascan palm – it thrives being a little pot-
bound. This species will be happiest in a warm, bright position
surrounded by good air movement, as it is prone to mildew (see
page 140) especially towards the end of summer. Move your
plant outdoors in summer, and bring it back indoors in autumn.

HOW TO GROW

Water well in summer, then gradually less so that towards the
end of autumn watering has ceased, when the plant begins to
go dormant. Keep plants completely dry in winter. In spring,
give a few light waterings to encourage Madagascan palm to
come back into growth. Feed once a month in summer with a
balanced fertilizer. Repotting is rarely required and should be
done only when pot-bound. Remove older yellowing leaves as
well as any leaves that show signs of mildew. Propagate from
seed soaked in water overnight before being sown (see page 34).

GROWING TIP

When moving your plant to a different location, such as from
indoors to outdoors, try to keep the same orientation to the
light, to prevent the stems from twisting.

ANOTHER NOTABLE SPECIES

• *P. saundersii* (kudu lily) is smaller and bushy and
produces pink flowers in spring.

LOOKING TO THE NORTH
Another *Pachypodium* species –
P. namaquanum – always leans
towards the north, giving it a
human-like form. By facing north,
it maximizes sunlight in winter
and shades itself from the
midday summer sun.

Pachypodium namaquanum

Recycled pallet planter

This project uses an old pallet that was repurposed to create this unique planter; however, a few boards from your local hardware shop will do just as well. It does not require any specialized woodworking tools or skills, and how you finish it is up to you – leave it natural, stain it or paint it.

Such a planter is a wonderful way of displaying your favourite succulents, especially when space is at a premium. It is narrow enough to fit neatly on a bright windowsill, and you could move it on to the dining table as a centrepiece when you have guests.

Select a few plants that work well visually together and that have similar water and light requirements. You may decide to keep the planting simple by using only a few specimens, where you can appreciate each one's individual form. Alternatively, why not position them close together, so they form a plant community. Play around with different forms, shapes and layouts to come up with your own unique design. However, be careful not to overplant, to avoid some plants crowding out others.

YOU WILL NEED
- 3 pieces, 45cm/18in long, of sawn timber, 9cm/3½in wide by 1.5cm/½in thick
- 2 pieces, 13cm/5in long, of sawn timber, 9cm/3½in wide by 1.5cm/½in thick
- Saw
- Electric drill and drill bits for wood
- Panel pin nails
- Wood glue
- Glasspaper
- Waterproofing wood sealant
- Wood stain or varnish (optional)
- Aggregate
- Cactus and succulent potting compost
- Soft brush
- A choice of succulents
- Fine grit topdressing

1. Cut a few pieces of timber to size. Drill drainage holes along the length of one piece of longer timber; this will be the bottom of the planter.
2. Assemble the timber pieces together with panel pin nails and some wood glue.
3. Sand down any rough sides and edges, using glasspaper.
4. Seal the inside of the planter with a waterproofing sealant, and, if desired, stain and varnish the outside.
5. Place a drainage layer of aggregate in the bottom of the planter, then some cactus and succulent potting compost.
6. Gently tease away any loose soil from the root ball of each plant.
7. Insert the first plant into the planter.
8. Continue placing your succulents (here, *Kalanchoe tomentosa*, *Haworthiopsis attenuata* and *Parodia leninghausii*).
9. Using a brush, clear away any potting mix from the succulents and sides of the planter.
10. Then topdress with fine grit and clean the plants again. Leave for a week or two, then water cautiously.

Balloon cactus

Parodia magnifica

The balloon cactus is a rewarding plant that can put on growth relatively quickly when conditions are favourable. Over time, it develops multiple, large, rounded heads and can form clumps. In summer, it produces clusters of bright yellow flowers, 4–5cm/1½–2in across, at the apex of each stem. It grows in rocky grassland in Brazil, often under deciduous shrubs in well-drained soils protected by leaf litter.

—

WHERE TO GROW

Plant in a mix of three parts soil-based potting compost, one part sharp sand, one part potting grit and one part sifted composted bark. Balloon cactus is ideal for a bright windowsill or conservatory. Move it outdoors in summer, and back indoors in autumn, to avoid wet and frosty weather.

—

HOW TO GROW

This species tolerates a bit more water than other cacti. Water well in spring and summer, but ensure the compost dries out completely before watering again. In autumn, reduce watering, and in winter water only lightly, if your plant looks a little dehydrated. Repot every 2–3 years. Propagate from stem cuttings (see page 37).

—

GROWING TIP

Keep balloon cactus cool (10–12°C/50–54°F) and dry in winter, to encourage flowering in summer.

Family
Cactaceae

Height and spread
30x15cm/12x6in

Temperature
10–28°C/50–82°F

Position
Bright, indirect light

Flowering time
Summer

Pests
Mealybug, red spider mite

THREATENED WITH EXTINCTION
Balloon cactus occurs in only a very limited area in Brazil, where it is considered to be at risk of extinction. Luckily, it is fairly common in cultivation.

OTHER NOTABLE SPECIES
- *P. leninghausii* (golden ball cactus) is endemic to Brazil and is covered with harmless golden bristles (see also Recycled pallet planter, page 114).
- *P. ottonis* is a small clumping species that is easy to grow and flowers freely in summer.

Cranesbill

Pelargonium paniculatum

Unlike the typical cultivated *Pelargonium*, this slow-growing cranesbill is one of a few species with succulent arborescent stems and summer-deciduous leaves; it eventually forms a multi-stemmed shrub. In late winter and spring, the leaves begin to shrivel, and the flowering stems then bear a mass of dainty pink flowers. This species grows naturally in arid and rocky areas of the Richtersveld in South Africa and in Namibia.

—

WHERE TO GROW

Grow in nutrient-poor, sandy soil with added potting grit or pumice, for drainage: for example, in a mix of one part soil-based potting compost, one part potting grit or pumice and one part sharp sand. Plant in a terracotta pot in a conservatory or greenhouse. Protect from summer rainfall.

—

HOW TO GROW

Keep dry during the summer dormancy period. In autumn, water lightly to encourage growth. In winter, increase the amount of water, being sure to allow the compost to dry out between waterings. By spring, as temperatures start to increase, reduce watering to allow the plant to go dormant. Feed monthly with a half-strength, low-nitrogen fertilizer during the growing season. Give an occasional prune, if straggly. Keep your plant a little bit pot-bound and repot in autumn only when it has outgrown the pot – generally every 3–5 years. Propagate by stem cuttings in autumn (see page 37), allowing each cutting to callus before inserting into silica sand. Sow seed in autumn (see page 34).

—

GROWING TIP

Once the leaves have dropped, retain the persistent leaf stalks as these add to the character of the plant.

—

OTHER NOTABLE SPECIES

- *P. echinatum* has prickly succulent stems and red-blotched, white flowers.
- *P. gibbosum* produces knobbly, jointed, succulent stems and greenish yellow flowers.

Family
Geraniaceae

Height and spread
1x0.5m/3x1½ft

Temperature
10–28°C/50–82°F

Position
Bright, indirect light

Flowering time
Late winter–spring

Pests
Caterpillar, mealybug, whitefly

SELF PLANTING SEEDS
Each *Pelargonium* seed has a long, twisted, feathery awn attached, to aid dispersal by the wind. When safely on the ground and wet, the awn begins to uncoil and drill the seed into the moist soil, where hopefully it germinates.

Blue torch cactus

Pilosocereus pachycladus

The blue torch cactus is an extremely attractive, columnar species with blue-grey, ribbed stems that are lined with spiny areoles bearing soft golden hairs. The stems need to reach at least 2m/7ft tall before they are crowned by short-lived, whitish, funnel-shaped, nocturnal flowers, which bats pollinate. Blue torch cactus is endemic to Brazil, where it grows in rocky soils among woody scrub.

—

WHERE TO GROW

Requires well-drained, slightly acidic potting compost so use equal parts of sifted composted bark, soil-based potting compost, sharp sand and potting grit. Plant in a pot that is large enough to encourage root growth, and position in a heated greenhouse or conservatory or on a warm bright windowsill. Blue torch cactus needs bright light, especially as it matures.

—

HOW TO GROW

Keep completely dry from mid-autumn through winter. Water often in spring and summer, ensuring the compost dries out before rewatering, as blue torch cactus is susceptible to rotting if overwatered (se page 141). Apply a monthly low-nitrogen fertilizer from spring to late summer. If your plant is getting too tall for its location, prune back the stem to encourage branching. Use the removed piece of stem to grow a new plant (see Stem cuttings, page 37).

—

GROWING TIP

Be sure to repot blue torch cactus before it becomes too pot-bound, to sustain growth.

ANOTHER NOTABLE SPECIES

- *P. leucocephalus* (old man cactus, woolly torch) has white-haired areoles covering its stems.

Family	
Cactaceae	
Height and spread	
5–10x1–5m/16–33x3–16ft	
Temperature	
12–28°C/54–82°F	
Position	
Bright light	
Flowering time	
Summer	
Pests	
Mealybug, red spider mite, scale insect	

THE DEEP BLUE
Blue torch cactus is often sold under the synonym *azureus*, meaning a deep blue colour.

Elephant bush

Portulacaria afra

This evergreen shrubby succulent is superficially similar to *Crassula ovata* (see page 72), except that it has smaller succulent leaves and reddish stems, especially when young. It is shy to flower, but when it does it produces a dainty pink bouquet. It is native to South Africa, Mozambique and Kenya, where it grows in rocky coastal thickets on the east coast. As its common name suggests, it is a favoured treat for elephants.

WHERE TO GROW

Grow in a potting mix of equal parts soil-based potting compost, potting grit, sharp sand and sifted composted bark. Potted plants can be moved outdoors in summer and back indoors during the colder months.

HOW TO GROW

In spring and summer, water well and feed monthly with a low-nitrogen fertilizer. Allow the potting soil to dry out between watering. Water sparingly in winter. Repot only when elephant bush is pot-bound. It responds well to pruning and shaping, so is a great candidate for a succulent bonsai (see page 44). Propagate by stem cuttings (see page 37), taking larger than normal ones if you prefer.

GROWING TIP

To avoid elephant bush aborting some of its branches, ensure you water when your plant is dry.

Family
Didiereaceae

Height and spread
1.5–5mx1–2m/
5–16x3–7ft

Temperature
12–28°C/54–82°F

Position
Bright light–semi-shade

Flowering time
Spring–summer

Pests
Mealybug

WATER THIEF
In its natural habitat, elephant bush is parasitized by a mistletoe, *Viscum crassulae*. This parasitic lifestyle is a great adaptation to drought – when water is scarce, steal it.

NOTABLE FORM
- *P. afra* f. *prostrata* is a creeping form suitable for a hanging basket (see page 58).

What is a planter?

Succulents are well adapted to growing in shallow soils and can withstand periods of drought, making them ideal candidates for various unusual planters. Small ones, whether they be recycled tins or large shells, make great party favours, gifts and table decorations. From teacups to treasure chests, if a container holds soil succulents can be grown in it! A few stylish cachepots also go well on a windowsill or in a conservatory.

When choosing a planter, bear in mind that your plant will need to be watered, and that planters with drainage holes will allow excess water to run out of the bottom. If you are using a planter that does not have any drainage holes, consider adding them if possible, or use an inner plastic pot, which can be removed when the plant needs to be watered. If neither of these options is available, water your planter cautiously, to avoid your plant becoming waterlogged.

Planting up and displaying your succulents in such planters can be a very creative process. The options and combinations are endless. Fill your chosen planter with an appropriate succulent potting compost (see page 26). Having planted your succulents, you might also decide to topdress around them with a decorative gravel.

A. *Astrophytum asterias* 'Super Kabuto'
B. *Crassula socialis* and *Espotoa lanata*
C. *Echeveria* sp.
D. *Euphorbia ritchiei* (aka *Monadenium ritchiei*)
E. *Gymnocalycium* sp.
F. *Mammillaria perezdelarosae* and *Pachyphytum hookeri*
G. *Rebutia* sp.

Fire crown cactus

Rebutia minuscula

This little cactus can be an extremely rewarding plant to grow. Given time, it produces multiple, globular, spine-covered heads. In spring, a mass of orange-red flowers may almost cover the whole plant. In its native habitat of Argentina, fire crown cactus grows at 1,200–1,500m/4,000–5,000ft in dry rocky outcrops, where it experiences cool, dry winters.

—

WHERE TO GROW

Plant in a free-draining sandy cactus mix such as equal parts soil-based potting compost, potting grit and sharp sand, in a small, shallow pot in a frost-free greenhouse or on a bright windowsill. In midsummer, move it outdoors out of direct sunlight or give it lots of ventilation. Bring it indoors in early autumn. See also What is a planter?, page 120.

—

Family	Cactaceae
Height and spread	5x12cm/2x5in
Temperature	5–25°C/41–77°F
Position	Bright light
Flowering time	Spring
Pests	Mealybug, red spider mite

BUMPY SKIN
Rebutia has small bumps, known as tubercles, instead of the more common cactus characteristic of ribs. The spines are held on an areole at the tip of each tubercle.

Aylostera deminuta syn. *Rebutia pulvinosa*

HOW TO GROW

In spring, water lightly, then increase the amount in summer, ensuring the compost dries out between waterings. During the hottest days of summer, give a more regular light watering, to keep fire crown cactus cool, but be careful not to saturate the compost. Feed monthly in spring and summer with a half-strength, low-nitrogen fertilizer. Reduce watering in autumn, and in winter keep the compost dry. Misting will help reduce red spider mite infestations (see page 139). Repot every 2–3 years into a slightly larger, shallow pot. Propagate by division of offsets (see page 39) or by seed (see page 34).

GROWING TIP

If growing fire crown cactus indoors, ensure it has night temperatures of 5–10°C/41–50°F and keep it dry over winter, to encourage flowering in spring.

NOTABLE HYBRIDS
- *R.* 'Alex' has bicoloured, white and pink petals.
- *R.* 'Amelie' produces bright pink flowers.
- *R.* 'Apricot Ice' bears orange flowers fading to apricot.

Mistletoe cactus

Rhipsalis baccifera

The leafless, almost spineless mistletoe cactus is a widespread, very variable species with five recognized subspecies. It grows naturally as an epiphyte hanging from the tree branches in humid forests or occasionally growing from rock cliffs. Dainty white flowers form along the long, thin, green, pendent stems; they then develop into semi-translucent, round, edible berries not dissimilar to that of a mistletoe.

—

WHERE TO GROW

Mistletoe cactus is ideal for growing in a hanging basket (see page 58) or a pot where stems can trail over the sides. It is cold sensitive so grow indoors in cold climates; it makes an excellent house plant. This species likes a nutrient-rich, free-draining mix: for example, a combination of one part orchid bark, one part perlite and two parts multipurpose potting compost.

—

HOW TO GROW

If you live in a hard-water area, use filtered water or rainwater instead of tap water. Mistletoe cactus needs regular watering and frequent misting in spring and summer; however, be careful not to oversaturate the soil. In autumn and winter, water more sparingly. Feed monthly with a foliar fertilizer in summer. Repot as soon as the potting mix starts to lose its structure. Propagate from seed (see page 34) or from stem cuttings, 5–7cm/2–3in long (see page 37) in spring and summer, planted into a mix of two parts coir and one part perlite; keep moist but not saturated with regular misting.

—

GROWING TIP

Mistletoe cactus needs a dry, cool period for a month before it flowers.

—

OTHER NOTABLE SPECIES AND SUBSPECIES
- *R. baccifera* subsp. *horrida* is a subspecies covered with soft, hair-like spines.
- *R. paradoxa* (mouse tail cactus) develops strange, almost twisted stems.

Family
Cactaceae
Height and spread
4x1m/13x3ft
Temperature
5–28°C/41–82°F
Position
Semi-shade
Flowering time
Spring
Pests
Mealybug

HOW DID IT GET THERE?
Rhipsalis baccifera is the only cactus species said to occur naturally outside the Americas, as it is also native to tropical regions of Africa, Mauritius, Madagascar and Sri Lanka.

Christmas cactus

Schlumbergera truncata aka flor de maio (May flower)

This is one of seven *Schlumbergera* species all native to Brazil, where it lives in the tropical coastal forests as an epiphyte growing in the trees, or on rocks as a lithophyte. The leaflike segments are actually flattened stems known as cladodes. When healthy, this species will reward you with an abundance of cascading, pink-red flowers around Christmastime in the northern hemisphere.

WHERE TO GROW

Plant in a free-draining, fine-barked orchid compost in a hanging basket (see page 58) positioned near a window or in a conservatory. In summer, move the pot outdoors into a shaded location.

Family	
Cactaceae	
Height and spread	
50x50cm/20x20in	
Temperature	
10–28°C/50–82°F	
Position	
Bright, indirect light	
Flowering time	
Early winter	
Pests	
Mealybug, red spider mite, scale insect	

FAMILY TREE
Schlumbergera truncata was first described in 1819, from a specimen growing in Kew's collection. It is one of the parents of the many hybrids available today, with *S. russelliana* the other parent.

Schlumbergera × buckleyi

HOW TO GROW

Water well in spring and summer; do not to let the compost stay wet, or else rot may occur. In autumn and winter, water only when Christmas cactus is wilting or the compost is very dry. Provide high humidity in the growing season, by regularly misting or by placing the plant over a tray of pebbles and water. Feed monthly with a balanced fertilizer during the growing season. Repot every 2–3 years, either in a same-sized pot or a slightly larger one. Don't be tempted to overpot as this could lead to the compost staying wet and causing root rot (see page 141). Propagate from stem cuttings, 1–3 segments long (see page 37); once its wound has healed, pot each cutting into a mix of two parts coir and one part perlite or into a fine-barked orchid compost.

—

GROWING TIP

If you are growing Christmas cactus as an indoor plant, give it night temperatures of 10–12°C/50–54°F in autumn, to encourage better flowering.

ANOTHER NOTABLE GENUS
- *Hatiora salicornioides* (Dancing bones cactus) has strange, bottle-like, segmented stems.

Burro's tail

Sedum morganianum

Burro's tail is native to Mexico, where it hangs from cliffs in tropical deciduous forests. Its pendulous stems bear cylindrical, blue-grey leaves pointed at the tips. Reddish, star-shaped flowers form in spring and summer.

—

WHERE TO GROW

Plant in a free-draining potting mix with a small amount of organic matter, such as one part soil-based potting compost, one part potting grit, one part sharp sand and one part sifted composted bark. Grow in a hanging basket (see page 58) or in a decorative pot where burro's tail can trail off a window ledge. Move it outdoors in summer; and bring indoors again before there is a risk of frost.

—

HOW TO GROW

Water well in spring and summer, allowing the soil to dry out before rewatering. In autumn and winter, water lightly only when necessary. Feed monthly with a low-nitrogen fertilizer in the growing season. Plants will thrive in a hanging basket for many years and will not need to be repotted. Propagate from leaf cuttings (see page 38) or from stem cuttings (see page 37) if you want a bigger plant sooner.

—

GROWING TIP

Avoid touching burro's tail too much as leaves can fall off easily, resulting in bald spots on the stems.

Family	
Crassulaceae	
Height and spread	
5x60cm/2x24in	
Temperature	
5–28°C/41–82°F	
Position	
Bright light	
Flowering time	
Spring–summer	
Pests	
Aphid, mealybug, scale insect	

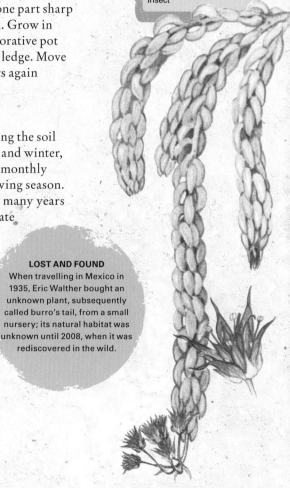

LOST AND FOUND
When travelling in Mexico in 1935, Eric Walther bought an unknown plant, subsequently called burro's tail, from a small nursery; its natural habitat was unknown until 2008, when it was rediscovered in the wild.

OTHER NOTABLE SPECIES
- *S. adolphi* develops copper-toned leaves when exposed to high light levels (see also Green wall, page 70).
- *S. burrito* has fat, fleshy, rounded leaves.

Growing from leaves

Growing new plants from leaves is a great way of getting large numbers of new plants from one plant, and you can then share them with your friends. Most members of the Crassulaceae family are very easy to grow in this way, so if you have any such plants, why not try taking leaf cuttings.

In their natural habitats, many succulent species propagate naturally by leaves. These fall off the mother plant and land in a rocky crevice, where if conditions are favourable they can root and grow into new plants. Succulent leaves can also drop into neighbouring pots and start growing at the bases of other plants. Some species even form new plantlets while still on the plant, like the very successful mother of thousands (*Kalanchoe daigremontiana*).

If you do give leaf propagation a go, do it in spring with healthy plump leaves that are not too old. Soon you will have a small army of new succulent babies.

SUCCULENTS SUITABLE FOR GROWING FROM LEAVES
Adromischus
Echeveria
Gasteria
Graptopetalum
Kalanchoe
Pachyphytum
Sedum

1. Select a suitable plant (here, *Pachyphytum hookeri*) to propagate. Carefully remove some plump healthy leaves cleanly from the stem.
2. Fill up a seed tray or pot with a sandy succulent potting compost. Then lightly moisten. Space the leaves out with the base of each leaf sitting just into the compost.
3. Place in a cool, dry spot out of direct sunlight. After a week, lightly spray over the leaves occasionally. Eventually, your leaves will root and produce new plantlets.
4. Once big enough, pot them up individually. The original leaves will gradually wither.

Queen of the night

Selenicereus grandiflorus

This species is one of the many night-flowering cacti given the common name queen of the night. It is a scandent (climbing) plant with long, grey-green, spiny stems. Its true beauty lies in its large, white-yellow, short-lived flowers, often borne en masse. Their sweet fragrance attracts bat and moth pollinators. It is native to South America and the Caribbean Islands, where it grows among rocks or scrambles up trees as a hemiepiphyte.

—

WHERE TO GROW

Plant in a free-draining cactus compost with added organic matter: for example, use one part soil-based potting compost, one part potting grit and one part sifted composted bark. Queen of the night needs a support to scramble up or else grow it in a hanging basket (see page 58) indoors or in a greenhouse. Position in some bright light in spring, to encourage flowering. This species can grow quickly, so ensure it has adequate space.

—

Family	Cactaceae
Height and spread	5–10x2m/16–33x7ft
Temperature	5–28°C/41–82°F
Position	Bright, indirect light–semi-shade
Flowering time	Summer
Pests	Mealybug, red spider mite

EDIBLE FRUITS
The red or yellow fruits of many species closely related to *S. grandiflorus* are edible, and some – referred to as dragon fruit – are very ornate and exotic-looking.

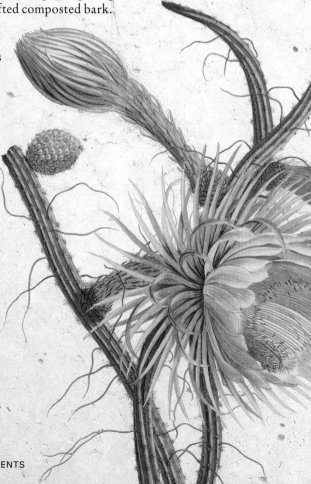

HOW TO GROW

This cactus tolerates a little more water than many other cactus, especially in the growing season. If the weather is warm and sunny, a weekly watering should be enough, but be sure to let the compost dry out before watering again. In winter, give only a light watering if your plant looks a little thirsty. Feed monthly in the growing season with a low-nitrogen fertilizer. Propagate from stem cuttings (see page 37) in summer or by seed (see page 34).

GROWING TIP

A well-established root system is needed to encourage flowers, so give your plant a big enough pot to allow for root growth.

ANOTHER NOTABLE SPECIES

- *S. validus* (moonlight cactus) is shorter and is a great plant for a hanging basket.

Cobweb houseleek

Sempervivum arachnoideum

Cobweb houseleek is a strange, clump-forming, evergreen succulent nicknamed after its cobweb-like hairs, which cover each rosette of red-flushed, green leaves. Bright pink flowers emerge from the centre of each rosette on a thick flowering stalk. This species grows naturally in rocky areas with shallow soil, high up in the Alps, Apennines and Carpathian mountains.

—

WHERE TO GROW

This cold-hardy succulent thrives in well-drained, loamy soil in a rock garden (see page 88) or crevice garden – or else on a green roof or in the cracks of a rock wall (see also Green wall, page 70). It makes a great plant for a shallow pot, too. Plant it in a mix of two parts soil-based potting compost and one part potting grit. Before winter, pots can be moved into a protected spot or greenhouse, so they don't get too much rain.

—

FLOWERS TO DIE FOR
Cobweb houseleek is monocarpic, which means the flowering stem comes from the terminal bud of the rosette, which dies after flowering. Luckily, this plant produces many offsets to take its place.

Family	
Crassulaceae	
Height and spread	
10x30cm/4x12in	
Temperature	
–15–28°C/5–82°F	
Position	
Bright light–semi-shade	
Flowering time	
Summer	
Pests	
Aphid, vine weevil	

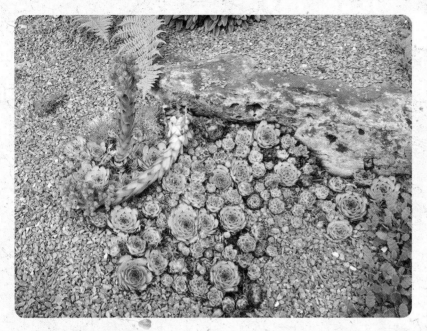

Sempervivum calcareum

HOW TO GROW

Cobweb houseleek is a hassle-free plant to grow and does not require frequent repotting. Water well from spring to autumn; keep drier in winter. Feed monthly in summer with a low-nitrogen fertilizer. Propagate by division of offsets (see page 39).

—

GROWING TIP

When growing outdoors, plant cobweb houseleek in a well-drained raised bed or rock garden, to help it cope with winter rain.

ANOTHER NOTABLE SPECIES
- *S. calcareum* has distinctive, red-tipped leaves.

Starfish plant

Stapelia grandiflora

This slowly creeping succulent with angular, square stems is mat-forming. It is native to southern Africa, where it grows in dry areas, often at the bases of larger nurse plants or among rocks where it is out of direct sunlight. When it comes into flower, each large, solitary, egg-like bud splits open, revealing a hairy, starfish-like bloom.

—

WHERE TO GROW

Grow this shallow-rooted plant in a shallow pot with enough room for it to creep. It needs a free-draining mix with a small amount of well-composted organic matter: for example, one part sand, one part potting grit and one part sifted composted bark. Position on a windowsill or in a conservatory, in partial shade, especially in midsummer. See also South African mini-desert, page 106.

—

Family
Apocynaceae

Height and spread
25x30cm/10x12in

Temperature
10–28°C/50–82°F

Position
Bright, indirect light–semi-shade

Flowering time
Summer

Pests
Mealybug

ART OF THE TRICKSTER
The flowers of starfish plant are said to mimic rotting meat. Its red flowers and pungent scent trick fly pollinators into thinking they have found a suitable place to lay their eggs.

Orbea verrucosa

HOW TO GROW

Water sparingly in winter, and increase the amount of water from spring to autumn. Water well in the growing season, but give the compost time to dry out before rewatering; if in doubt, wait until the stems start to feel soft – starfish plant is very prone to root rot (see page 141). Feed monthly with a half-strength, low-nitrogen fertilizer during the growing season. Repotting is needed only infrequently, when the starfish plant has outgrown its pot. Propagate from stem cuttings (see page 37) or by layering (see page 39).

GROWING TIP

Keep a watchful eye for mealybugs (see page 138), which like to hide between the compost and the stem. Mealybug infestation will quickly lead to secondary rot if left unchecked.

ANOTHER NOTABLE GENUS
- *Orbea variegata* is a close relative and a bit smaller, at 8–10cm/3¼–4in high, but has equally pungent, red-flecked, yellow flowers.

Troubleshooting

General hygiene practices such as removing dead leaves and dying flowers can reduce pests and diseases. Keep your plants and greenhouse weed-free and clean any staging areas regularly. Use a disinfectant on benches, tools and hosepipes.

This *Parodia* has succumbed to black rot. Dispose of infected material to minimize its spread.

PESTS

The best form of pest control is prevention. Be sure to inspect thoroughly any new plants coming into your collection and then quarantine them, keeping them separate from the rest of your collection until you are certain they are pest-free. If you spot any pests, remove them as soon as possible, and move the plant away from others to reduce the risk of the attack spreading. Watch out for rodents, slugs and snails, which are a particular problem when growing plants outdoors, as well as for the following pests.

Aloe mites

Aloes are susceptible to aloe mites, which cause cancer-like growths. They are very difficult to eradicate, but you could try treating them with a systemic insecticide; in the worst-case scenario, burn infected plants.

Ants

Although not a direct pest to succulent plants, ants are farmers of honeydew-producing pests such as aphids (see below), mealybugs (see page 138) and scale insects (see page 140). They move these pests from plant to plant and help protect them from biological controls. The best method of control is ant bait, which the worker ants take back to the nest and feed to the queen.

Aphids

These insects can be found on the flowering stems of some succulents. The best form of control is to remove the flowering stem. There are many biological controls effective at controlling aphids: for example, parasitoid wasps like *Aphidius* spp.; predatory flies such as *Aphidoletes*; hoverflies; and ladybirds.

The aphids feeding on these *Adansonia* leaves are being parasitized by a beneficial wasp, *Aphidius*, while the small orange larvae are of *Aphidoletes*, a predatory fly.

Blue or yellow sticky traps can be used to catch and monitor pests such as fungus gnats. Blue traps also attract thrips while yellow ones lure whitefly, too.

Fungus gnats

Small black flies around the top of the compost are likely to be fungus gnats, also known as sciarid flies. As their name suggests, they are attracted by fungus in the soil, where they lay their eggs. When they are larvae, fungus gnats feed on fungus and later on fine roots. They are also attracted by root rot (see page 141)and can transfer rot spores from pot to pot. They can be problematic with new seedlings, but if you sterilize your compost and keep your pots covered with a propagator lid you can exclude fungus gnats. Control them with predatory mites such as *Hypoaspis miles* or *Atheta coriaria* (a predatory rove beetle).

Mealybugs

The No. 1 enemies of any succulent grower are these small, egg-shaped insects, which have a cotton-like appearance. They feed by piercing stems to suck plant sap, and they can multiply very quickly, so even a few can quickly

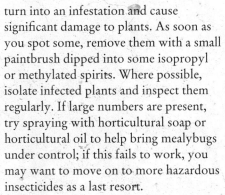

Ants protect mealybugs (here, on *Opuntia* new growth) from other pests and in return harvest secreted honeydew, a favourite food for ants.

Sometimes red spider mites cover apical growth (here, of *Adenium*) with webbing.

turn into an infestation and cause significant damage to plants. As soon as you spot some, remove them with a small paintbrush dipped into some isopropyl or methylated spirits. Where possible, isolate infected plants and inspect them regularly. If large numbers are present, try spraying with horticultural soap or horticultural oil to help bring mealybugs under control; if this fails to work, you may want to move on to more hazardous insecticides as a last resort.

Root mealybugs are a different species, and are smaller and not as woolly as mealybugs. They can be found on the roots of various plant species and often go undetected until the plant is repotted. Control root mealybugs by drenching the pot with a pesticide or by removing all the soil during repotting.

Red spider mite
These tiny red arachnids often feed on leaves and new growth and can go unnoticed until a leaf or growing point becomes silvered or mottled. With high numbers, fine webbing will be present. Red spider mites can cause significant, long-lasting damage, especially to slow-growing cacti. In spring and summer, keep a vigilant eye out for them, and associated damage, and as soon as you see them treat with horticultural soaps, horticultural oils or pesticides. With beneficial predators becoming more widely available, you may prefer to try releasing predatory mites such as *Amblyseius andersoni* and *A. californicus*, which help control the population.

Scale insects appear on stems (here, a columnar cactus) and then migrate up the plant.

Vine weevils
These blackish, long-snouted beetles cause notching on plant leaves in their adult phase. During their grub stage, however, vine weevils can cause significant root damage and burrow into the stems of some succulent plants. Use root drenches with pesticides to control infestations. Drenches with pathogenic nematodes or insect-killing entomopathogenic fungi are also available.

DISEASES

Any succulent collection is prone to fungal infections such as black spot, which are generally caused by cultural problems. The risk of fungal disease is reduced if you ensure good air movement around plants; are careful not to overwater; on dull days, avoid watering or getting plants wet; and use an appropriate potting medium (see Potting composts and soils, page 26, as well as plant profiles, pages 40–135).

Mildew
This fungal infection can occur on a range of leafy succulents such as *Adenium* and *Pachypodium*. It manifests itself as grey spots on the surfaces of the leaves that eventually spread. For heavy infections, remove the infected leaves, allow good air movement around the plant and keep the foliage dry. A fungicide can be used as a preventative measure.

Scale insects
These small, sap-sucking insects are typically covered by white, hemispherical, scale-like shells. A number of different scale species can be found on plant stems and leaves. For control, physically remove them with a paintbrush dipped into 70 per cent alcohol. After treatment, monitor your plants for reinfection.

Thrips
Thrips are small insects that often cause mottling and silvering in flowers and on leaves from spring through to autumn. To control them, remove affected flowers and leaves or spray plants with a pesticide. There are various biological controls such as *Amblyseius cucumeris*, a predatory mite that feeds on thrips. It will switch to eating pollen when the thrip population is low.

Avoid wetting leaves to minimize the spread of fungal infections such as black spot (here, on *Gasteria*).

Rot
If you do suffer from rot issues, remove infected plants and cut back to healthy tissue; then try to re-root your plant. Although fungicides can be used, they are often better as preventatives rather than curatives. Rots can be caused by a variety of pathogenic fungi and bacteria. Keep your growing area clean and periodically disinfect hoses and tools to minimize spread. Also, keep an eye out for fungus gnats (see page 138), they can be an early indicator of root rot.

OTHER PLANT PROBLEMS
Problems such as deficiencies can cause serious issues for cacti and succulents. Among the most prevalent are the following.

Inappropriate nutrition
Correct nutrition is vital for any plant. Weak plants not only suffer from poor growth and yellowing, but they are also more susceptible to pests and diseases. Succulents are generally not hungry plants, but using a good-quality, low-nitrogen general fertilizer with added micronutrients

This *Echinopsis oxygona* has turned yellow, because it has received too much direct sunlight.

during the growing season will keep your plants healthy (see Feeding, page 30). Apply the general fertilizer at half the recommended strength, as over-fertilizing can cause just as many problems as underfeeding. Alternatively, opt for a specially formulated cactus and succulent fertilizer.

Scorch
For many succulent species, too much light can cause yellowing and, in severe cases, irreversible tissue damage. Therefore, always ensure your plants are in the optimum light conditions for the time of year. Move yellow plants out of direct sunlight; in time, they should improve. Severe scorch is irreversible; however, new growth can be propagated to replace damaged plants or, in some cases, new growth can form healthy plants again.

Index

Brimming with creative inspiration, how-to projects, and useful information to enrich your everyday life, quarto.com is a favourite destination for those pursuing their interests and passions.

First published in 2023 by Frances Lincoln, an imprint of The Quarto Group.
One Triptych Place,
London, SE1 9SH
United Kingdom
T (0)20 7700 6700 F (0)20 7700 8066
www.Quarto.com

A catalogue record for this book is available from the British Library.

ISBN 978-0-7112-7714-4
eISBN 978-0-7112-7715-1

10 9 8 7 6 5 4 3 2 1

Typeset in Stempel Garamond and Univers
Design by Arianna Osti

Printed in China

Photographic acknowledgement

All photographs © Paul Rees except for:

1 Maria Orlova/Unsplash; 2 Lacey Williams/Unsplash; 8 Bobbi Gaukel/Unsplash; 40–1 Katie Burkhart/Unsplash; 57 The Book Worm/Alamy Stock Photo; 68 Florilegius/Alamy Stock Photo; 75 Darling Archive/Alamy Stock Photo; 98 History and Art Collection/Alamy Stock Photo; 108 Album/Alamy Stock Photo; 138 D. Kucharski K. Kucharska/Shutterstock

Author's acknowledgements

It has taken many hands, minds and people hours to bring this book to life.

I would like to thank Rosie for her support through the whole process of writing this book, especially when I seemed to be continually glued to my laptop and for helping set up and photograph the projects. It took a team to bring this book together, thanks must go to: Joanna Chisholm for all her work editing and ensuring we kept to schedule; Arianna Osti for her creative design, arranging the text and images; Pei Chu for helping source images for the plant profiles; Gina Fullerlove, Lydia White, Tony Hall and Michael Brunström for believing in me and giving me the opportunity to author this book. I would also like to say thank you to my friends, family and colleagues in the tropical nursery for supporting me.

Instagram: just_botanical
Twitter: @Paul_Rees_